Disney

Picture Dictionary

PaRragon

Bath · New York · Singapore · Hong Kong · Cologne · Delhi · Melbourne

Written by Thea Feldman and Alan Benjamin

This edition published by Parragon in 2009

Parragon
Queen Street House
4 Queen Street
Bath BA1 1HE, UK

ISBN 978-1-4075-6158-5
Printed in China

Dear Parent,

Disney's *Picture Dictionary* is designed to be an invaluable companion for young children, helping them to develop and use the vocabulary they need to describe their busy world. This book, packed with more than 900 words, will encourage children as they move through the different stages of early learning.

The book is organized alphabetically to help the youngest children find the everyday words and objects they meet. Each word is presented together with a friendly Disney picture to help the child understand its meaning. For a slightly older child, this is a true first dictionary, with easy-to-understand definitions for each word, together with a sentence showing its usage.

This is a book for the whole family to enjoy together, and for early readers to begin using on their own. Beloved Disney characters invite your child to turn to this book again and again to discover familiar words as well as those that encourage the imagination and fuel a young child's passion for learning!

a b c d e f g h i j k l m n o p q r s t u v w x y z

apple

Aa

accident

An accident is something that happens by mistake.

Only Goofy could have an **accident** like that!

acorn

An acorn is the hard nut of the oak tree.

The **acorn** is Chip 'n' Dale's favourite food.

above

When you are above something, you are on top of it or higher than it.

It's fun to fly **above** the clouds!

act

To act is to pretend to be someone or something that you're not.

Baloo loves to **act** silly.

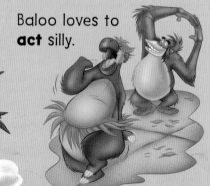

action

An action is something that you do.

Mushu can learn a lot by watching Mulan in **action**, doing karate.

actor

An actor is a person who pretends to be someone else in a film, a play or a TV programme.

Donald thinks he is a great **actor**.

adult

An adult is someone who has grown up.

> Simba, you're a young lion now, but soon you'll be an **adult**!

add

When you add something, you put it with another thing.

> Let's **add** more coins to my collection!

adventure

An adventure is something you do that is new and exciting.

Wendy and her brothers had quite an **adventure** with Peter Pan.

after

After means later than, or following.

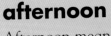

The toys are in a row **after** Andy's mum tidies up.

address

An address tells you where a building is or where someone lives. It can include a house number, street name, town, postcode and country.

Let's check the **address** of this letter!

aeroplane

An aeroplane is a machine with wings that can fly.

An **aeroplane** is the fastest way to travel!

afternoon

Afternoon means after 12 o'clock noon.

Lady and Tramp run in the park every **afternoon**.

9

agree

When people agree, it means that they think or feel the same way about something.

Let's **agree** to play with everything.

alarm clock

An alarm clock has a buzzer or bell that wakes you up.

Donald wakes up as soon as his **alarm clock** goes off!

alien

An alien is a living creature from another planet.

Hmm! Earth might be a good place for an **alien** to hide.

airport

An airport is a place where aeroplanes take off and land.

The **airport** is very busy!

all

All means every part of something.

All my hands are full! How many hands do you have?

alone

You are alone when you are by yourself.

When Lilo is **alone,** she likes to listen to her Elvis records.

also

Also means as well as, in addition to.

While she cleans, Cinderella **also** likes to sing.

amusement park

An amusement park is a place with rides and food. People go there to have fun.

I can see the whole **amusement park**.

answer

An answer is what you give to someone who asks a question.

Scuttle, you'll know the **answer**. What is this thing?

always

Always means all the time.

Baloo **always** scratches his back against a tree.

angry

When you get cross, you feel angry.

Calm down, you two! Don't be so **angry** with each other.

ant

An ant is a tiny crawling insect that is very strong.

Flik is a small **ant** with big ideas!

ambulance

An ambulance is a vehicle with a siren. It takes people who are ill to hospital.

An **ambulance** has flashing lights to warn other vehicles.

animal

An animal is any living thing that is not a plant.

Mufasa is an **animal** that lives in the jungle.

apple

An apple is the fruit that grows on an apple tree.

The evil Witch gave Snow White a poisoned **apple**.

a b c d e f g h i j k l m n o p q r s t u v w x y z

apron

An apron is something you wear over your clothes. It protects them while you cook.

It's OK if you spill something by accident on your **apron**.

around

Around means on all sides of something.

Simba chases Nala **around** the tree.

audience

An audience is a group of people who watch something.

The Aristocats enjoy making music for an **audience** of any size!

aquarium

An aquarium is a bowl or tank of water that holds fish and other sea creatures.

This cat can only watch the fish in the **aquarium**.

ask

When you ask something, you use words to form a question.

May I **ask** you to read to me?

aunt

An aunt is a sister of your father or mother, or the wife of your uncle.

I love being your **Aunt** Daisy.

armchair

An armchair is a big comfortable chair with arms.

I like to sit in a comfy **armchair** when I read a good book.

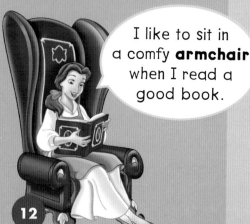

astronaut

An astronaut is someone who travels into outer space.

An **astronaut** wears a special suit.

avocado

An avocado is a green fruit that grows on a tree.

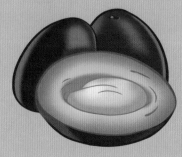

An **avocado** is very soft when it's ready to eat.

bear

Bb

back

The back of something is the part behind the front.

There is a swimming pool at the **back** of Mickey's house.

bad

When something is bad, it is not good.

Lucifer is a **bad** cat!

bag

A bag is a soft container that you use to carry things.

We carry our shopping home in a **bag**.

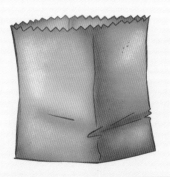

I've put my books in this **backpack**.

backpack

A backpack is a bag with straps. It goes over your shoulders and hangs down your back.

baby

A baby is a very young child.

What a strange-looking **baby**!

bacon

Bacon is dried meat from a pig. You slice bacon and fry it.

I think **bacon** smells so good when it's cooking!

bake

When you bake something, you cook it in an oven.

I'll be happy to **bake** that pie for you.

a
b
c
d
e
f
g
h
i
j
k
l
m
n
o
p
q
r
s
t
u
v
w
x
y
z

bakery

A bakery is a place where you buy fresh bread and other baked foods.

Mmmm! Smell the fresh bread at the **bakery**!

banana

A banana is a long yellow fruit that grows on a tree.

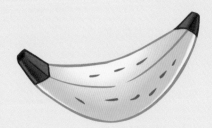

Abu can peel a **banana** very quickly to reach the fruit inside!

bandage

A bandage is a strip of cloth that you use to cover a wound.

It's good to cover a grazed knee with a **bandage**.

ball

A ball is a round object that you use to play many games.

Let's play catch with the **ball**!

band

A band is a group of musicians who play together.

We're the Under the Sea **Band**.

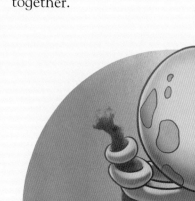

balloon

A balloon is a thin rubber bag that is blown up with air or gas.

The red **balloon** belongs to Daisy.

bank

A bank is a place where people keep their money.

There is a monster outside the **bank**.

bank

The bank of a river is the land on either side of the water.

There are daisies growing on the **bank** of the river.

barn

A barn is a building where farm animals live.

Cows and horses are some animals that live in a **barn**.

baseball

Baseball is a game where you hit a ball with a long thin bat.

Donald wants to have a go in every **baseball** game.

basketball

Basketball is a game where you throw a large round ball through a raised hoop.

You don't have to be tall to be good at **basketball**!

bass

A bass is a very big musical instrument with strings.

The Scat Cat Band uses the **bass** when its members play together.

bat

A bat is a stick that you use to hit a baseball.

When it's your turn, you have to swing the **bat** at just the right time!

bat

A bat is the biggest flying animal that is not a bird.

Bats are strange animals that can hang upside down.

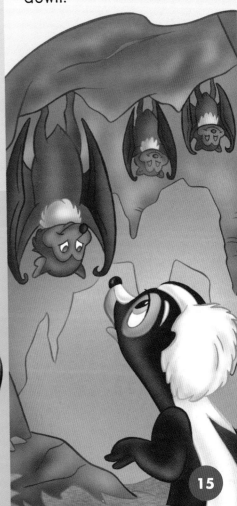

a
b
c
d
e
f
g
h
i
j
k
l
m
n
o
p
q
r
s
t
u
v
w
x
y
z

bath

A bath is the place where you wash yourself to get clean.

Playing in the bath can be fun!

bath

When you bath, you wash yourself and become clean.

If you don't mind, I like a little privacy when I bath!

bathroom

The bathroom is the room where you find a basin, a bath and a toilet in a home or a hotel.

Goofy likes to sing in the bathroom!

be

To be is to live or exist.

I'm a cute kitten now, and I will be a beautiful cat one day!

beach

A beach is the sandy area beside the sea.

Welcome to my beach! Grab a towel and enjoy the sun!

beach ball

A beach ball is a large colourful ball that you play with on the beach.

Lilo's lovely **beach ball** is bright pink and yellow.

beak

A beak is the hard, pointed part on the outside of a bird's mouth.

This toucan can crack open nuts in its big green **beak**.

bean

A bean is the seed of some kinds of plants.

Beans come in many shapes and colours.

bear

A bear is a big furry animal with sharp teeth and claws. A bear growls when it talks.

The only **bear** you should hug is your teddy bear!

beard

A beard is the hair that grows on a man's chin and cheeks.

To get King Triton's attention, Sebastian pulls on his **beard**.

bed

A bed is a piece of furniture that you sleep on.

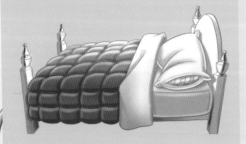

Does someone tuck you into **bed** every night?

bee

A bee is a flying insect. Some kinds of bee make honey.

Be careful! This **bee** might sting you.

beautiful

Something that is beautiful is lovely to look at.

Cinderella's gown is so **beautiful**!

become

Become means to change or grow into something new.

Sebastian wants to **become** the most honoured bandleader of all time!

bedroom

A bedroom is where you go to sleep at night.

One night, Wendy and her brothers saw a ship outside their **bedroom** window!

before

Before means earlier than something else.

The Dwarfs' cottage was messy **before** Snow White moved in.

below

Below means under or lower than something else.

Nala, you're above me, and I'm **below** you!

best

If something is the best, it means that there is nothing better.

Ariel, you are the **best** singer!

behind

Behind means at the back of.

Nala found Simba hiding **behind** the rock.

belt

A belt is a long narrow strip of leather or cloth that you wear around your waist.

Minnie was looking for a red **belt** to wear with her new dress.

bell

A bell is a hollow object that makes a ringing sound. Most bells are made of metal.

The **bell** rings every morning at the start of the school day.

bench

A bench is a narrow seat that you often find in a park.

This **bench** is a good place to sit and watch people in the park!

between

To be between something means to be in the middle of other things.

I am standing **between** Thumper and Bambi.

bicycle

A bicycle is something with two wheels, a seat and handlebars. You ride a bicycle by pushing on the pedals with your feet.

Donald can't win the race with that **bicycle**!

big

If something is big, it means that it takes up a lot of space.

Dumbo's ears are **big**, even for an elephant!

bird

A bird is an animal that has wings and feathers. Birds lay eggs.

Birds perch in the trees and sing in warm weather.

bird cage

A bird cage is a container with bars where a pet bird lives.

Only the finest **bird cage** will do for you, my pretty little birdie!

birthday party

You have a birthday party on the day of the year on which you were born.

Huey, Dewey and Louie share one big **birthday party**.

bite

When you bite something, you grab it with your teeth.

Puppies love to **bite** slippers!

blackboard

A blackboard is a hard board on which you draw and write with chalk.

The teacher uses the classroom **blackboard** every day.

blanket

A blanket is a soft cover for a bed.

Daisy loves a big cosy **blanket** to keep her warm on winter nights.

board game

A board game is a game for two or more players. The players move pieces around on a board marked with coloured areas.

Mickey loves to play this **board game** with his friends.

boat

A boat carries people and things across the water.

It's fun to take a **boat** ride.

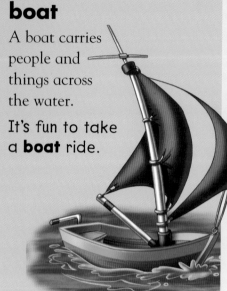

bone

Bones are one of the hard parts of someone's body that all together make up a skeleton. Many animals have bones.

Sniff! Sniff! Pluto's nose knows there's a meat **bone** nearby!

book

A book is something with pages and a cover that you read.

Belle reads a **book** whenever she can.

body

Your body is all of you, both inside and outside.

Can you find all the different parts of your **body**?

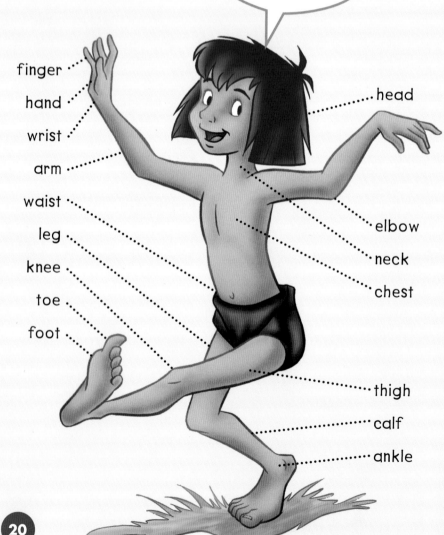

finger
hand
wrist
arm
waist
leg
knee
toe
foot

head
elbow
neck
chest
thigh
calf
ankle

bookcase

A bookcase is a piece of furniture with shelves. You keep your books in a bookcase.

Every **bookcase** that Belle has is full!

bookshop

A bookshop is a shop that sells books.

This **bookshop** has so many great things to read.

BOOKSHOP

boot

A boot is a shoe that covers the bottom part of your leg.

Splash! These **boots** will keep your feet dry in puddles.

bottle (baby's)

A baby drinks from a special bottle with a teat on it.

When you were a baby, did you drink milk from a **bottle**?

bowl

A bowl is a deep round dish that holds food.

Look at the colourful fruits in this pretty **bowl**!

bored

You are bored when you have nothing interesting to do.

Buzz is so **bored** when he's not with his friend Woody.

bottle

A bottle is a container that holds a liquid.

The Aristocats had a whole **bottle** of milk as a treat.

box

A box is a container that is usually in the shape of a square or a rectangle.

A pretty **box** like this should contain pretty things!

boring

Something is boring when it doesn't interest you.

Mortie and Ferdie think Mickey is teaching a **boring** subject.

boy

A boy is a child who will grow up to be a man.

John is the oldest **boy** in the Darling family.

a b c d e f g h i j k l m n o p q r s t u v w x y z

a
b
c
d
e
f
g
h
i
j
k
l
m
n
o
p
q
r
s
t
u
v
w
x
y
z

bread

Bread is a food that is baked. It is made from flour, water and eggs.

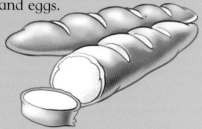

This **bread** is crusty on the outside and soft on the inside. *Yummy!*

bridge

A bridge joins together two pieces of land that are separated by water.

Maid Marian, thank you for this walk across the **bridge**.

break

When you break something, it falls to pieces or stops working.

May hopes her new vase won't **break** like the old one.

bring

If you bring something, you carry it with you when you go somewhere.

Gosh, next time it rains I'll **bring** a better umbrella!

broccoli

Broccoli is a green vegetable that looks like a little tree.

Broccoli is crunchy when you eat it raw.

breakfast

Breakfast is the first meal of the day.

Donald should eat his **breakfast,** not wear it!

broom

A broom is a long stick with a brush at the end of it. You use a broom to sweep things.

This is a magic **broom** – it's carrying buckets of water!

brother

If you have a brother, he is the boy child of your parents.

Come here, little **brother**. It's time for bed!

butter

Butter is a soft food that is made from milk or cream.

Mmmm! Let's spread this **butter** on some hot, fresh bread.

build

When you build something, you make it by putting pieces together.

What else can I **build** for Belle?

bus

A bus is a long vehicle with lots of seats and windows. It carries people from place to place.

Let's sit upstairs on the double-decker **bus**.

butterfly

A butterfly is a flying insect that has colourful wings.

A **butterfly** will flutter past you in the spring.

building

A building is a place with walls and a roof. People live or work in a building.

There are a lot of tall **buildings** in a city.

butcher

A butcher is someone who cuts up meat and sells it in a shop.

The **butcher** sells chicken, steak and other kinds of meat in his shop.

buy

When you buy something, you pay money for it so that it can belong to you.

I will never let you **buy** my Dalmatians!

a
b
c
d
e
f
g
h
i
j
k
l
m
n
o
p
q
r
s
t
u
v
w
x
y
z

a b c d e f g h i j k l m n o p q r s t u v w x y z

cake

A cake is a sweet, baked food. It is made from flour, sugar, butter and other things.

Minnie baked this **cake** for Daisy's birthday party.

camel

A camel is an animal that lives in the desert. It has one or two humps on its back.

This **camel** is looking for Aladdin. Have you seen him?

cat

calculator

A calculator is a machine that you use to add, subtract, multiply and divide.

I need a **calculator** to add up all my Elvis records.

camera

A camera is a machine that you use to take photographs.

Smile for the **camera**, Boo!

cabbage

A cabbage is a green vegetable that you cook or eat raw.

This **cabbage** looks like a big green flower!

call

To call means to speak in a loud voice to get someone's attention, or to telephone someone.

Minnie loves to **call** her friends.

can

If you can do something, it means that you are able to do it.

Can you swing from a tree like this monkey, Tarzan?

card

A card is a thick piece of paper, often with words and pictures on it.

Minnie has received a lovely long **card** from her pen friend.

candle

A candle is a stick of wax with a wick that burns and gives you light.

Make a wish and blow out the **candles**!

cap

A cap is a soft hat with a peak at the front.

Have you got a favourite **cap**?

candlestick

A candlestick is a holder for one or more candles.

I am the brightest **candlestick** of all!

car

A car is a vehicle with four wheels and an engine. A car's engine is powered by petrol or electricity.

Cruella De Vil is in her **car**, looking for Dalmatian puppies!

card (playing)

A playing card is a thick piece of rectangular paper with a number and shapes on it. Playing cards come in a set and are used for games.

Mickey and Donald get together every week to play **cards**.

carpet

A carpet is a covering for a floor.

Wow! This **carpet** really can fly!

catch

When you catch something, you grab it as it is moving.

It's hard to know which ball to **catch** first!

carrot

A carrot is a vegetable. It is the long orange root of the carrot plant.

Rabbits love to eat crunchy **carrots**.

castle

A castle is a large building with thick stone walls and tall towers.

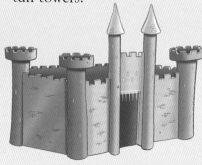

Every princess has at least one **castle** to live in!

cauliflower

A cauliflower is a large, round, bumpy-looking vegetable.

A **cauliflower** is a white and green vegetable that's good for you to eat.

carry

When you carry something, you hold it while you take it somewhere.

Daisy helps Donald to **carry** her presents.

cat

A cat is a pet animal that can purr and miaow.

Figaro is Geppetto's **cat**.

ceiling

The ceiling is the top part of the room.

It looks as if that ship might touch the **ceiling** if it comes through the window!

celery

Celery is a crunchy, stringy green vegetable.

Snap! That's the sound fresh **celery** makes as you break off a piece.

chair

A chair is a piece of furniture that you sit on.

Belle sits in a comfy **chair** when she's reading a good book.

change

When you change something, you make it different from the way it was before.

Come along, dear. **Change** your dress!

cello

A cello is a musical instrument with strings. It looks like a huge violin.

This **cello** belongs to the Scat Cat Band.

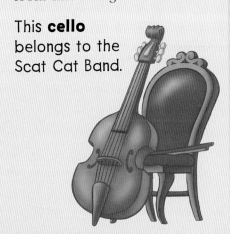

chalk

Chalk is a stick of coloured powder that you use to draw or write on a blackboard.

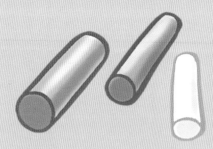

Teachers write on the blackboard with **chalk**.

chase

When you chase something, you try to catch it.

I'm going to **chase** you ... and catch you!

cereal

Cereal is a food that you eat for breakfast.

If you eat **cereal** with milk, it's a good way to start your day.

champion

A champion is the best person at doing a particular thing.

When it comes to scaring kids, Sulley is the **champion**!

SCARE TOTALS

1 SULLIVAN

2 RANDALL

cheese

Cheese is a soft or hard food that is made from the milk of cows, sheep or goats.

Gus just loves **cheese**!

a
b
c
d
e
f
g
h
i
j
k
l
m
n
o
p
q
r
s
t
u
v
w
x
y
z

cherry

A cherry is the round fruit that grows on a cherry tree.

A sweet **cherry** is a juicy summer treat.

child

A child is a young person who will grow up to be an adult.

As a **child,** Tarzan was friends with all kinds of animals.

chess

Chess is a game for two people. It is played with 32 pieces on a board with light and dark squares.

I am better at **chess** than you are!

children

Two or more young people are called children.

There are three **children** in the Darling family: Wendy, John and Michael.

chocolate

Chocolate is a sweet food made from cocoa beans and sugar.

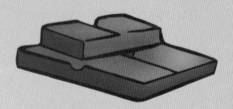

Let's unwrap a bar of **chocolate** and take a big bite!

chicken

A chicken is a bird that lives on a farm. People keep chickens for their eggs and their meat.

A **chicken** is a bird that doesn't fly very much.

choose

When you choose something, you pick it out from other things.

Mickey, let's **choose** the perfect tie.

28

circus

A circus is a show with clowns and acrobats. Sometimes there are animals in a circus.

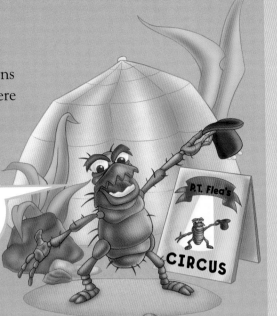

Come in and see the greatest flea **circus** in the world!

P.T. Flea's CIRCUS

clean

If something is clean, it is not dirty.

These Dalmatian puppies are all **clean** after their bath.

clap

You clap your hands together to show that you are pleased with something.

Clap, clap! They like Pinocchio's dancing.

classroom

A classroom is a room in a school where a teacher teaches pupils.

Everyone laughs in Goofy's **classroom**!

climb

When you climb, you use your hands and feet to take you higher.

Baloo helps Mowgli to **climb** the tree.

clarinet

A clarinet is a long thin musical instrument. You blow into it to make music.

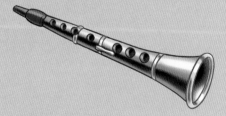

The Scat Cats really swing when they play the **clarinet**!

clean

When you clean something, you remove the dirt from it.

Oh, no! Cinderella will have to **clean** the floor again.

clock

A clock is a machine that tells us what time it is.

I'm one **clock** that's on time!

close

When you close something, such as a door, you shut it.

Donald tries hard to **close** the door.

coach

A coach is a person who teaches people how to do something better.

These players need a good **coach**!

coin

A coin is a round metal piece of money.

The only thing Uncle Scrooge likes better than a **coin** is five coins!

cloud

A cloud is a white shape in the sky. It is made up of millions of tiny raindrops.

Every **cloud** in the sky is a different shape.

coat

A coat is a piece of clothing that you wear over other clothes. A coat keeps you warm and dry.

Minnie's favourite **coat** has a big pink flower on it.

cold

When you have a cold, you sneeze a lot and you don't feel well.

Poor Minnie! She has a very bad **cold**!

clown

A clown is someone in a circus who wears funny clothes. Clowns do silly things to make people laugh.

The dog and the **clown** work together.

coffee

Coffee is a drink that is made from roasted coffee beans and hot water.

The smell of fresh **coffee** is delicious!

colour

When you colour something, you use crayons, felt-tip pens or paints.

I like to **colour** pictures of Stitch!

colour

A colour is one of the different shades in a rainbow, such as red, yellow or blue.

Pocahontas sees so many **colours** in the leaves.

green

orange

yellow

blue

black

purple

red

pink

brown

white

grey

comb

A comb is a flat piece of plastic with teeth. You use it to keep your hair tidy.

A **comb** feels good when it goes through your hair, doesn't it?

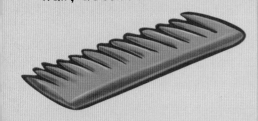

computer

A computer is a machine that you use to write letters, play games, send e-mails and do many other things.

Using a **computer** is so easy that even a puppy can do it!

concert

A concert is a time when musicians play for an audience.

Everyone dances at the Scat Cat Band's **concert**.

a b **c** d e f g h i j k l m n o p q r s t u v w x y z

cook

A cook is someone whose job is to cook food for other people to eat.

Sulley likes to **cook** spaghetti and meatballs!

costume

A costume is the clothing that you put on to look like someone else.

When Mickey puts on this **costume**, he becomes the Sorcerer's Apprentice.

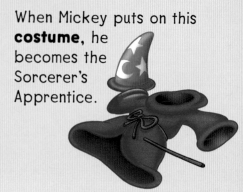

cook

When you cook food, you heat it up by boiling, baking or frying it.

It's fun to **cook** outdoors over a fire!

corner

A corner is the place where two walls or two streets meet.

The cats ran around the **corner** when they smelled the spilled milk!

cot

A cot is a bed for a baby or a young child. It has high sides.

Did you sleep in a **cot** like this when you were a baby?

corn

Corn is a vegetable with little rows of yellow seeds that grow on a tall, green plant.

When **corn** is freshly picked, it still has green leaves on it.

cost

The cost of something is how much money you have to pay for it.

This one **costs** less!

cough

When you cough, you try to clear your throat.

What do you think is making Goofy **cough**?

cow

A cow is a large farm animal that makes a mooing noise.

This **cow** has a large bell around her neck. Do you know why?

cracker

A cracker is a thin crispy biscuit made of flour and water. Crackers are not sweet.

Cheese and **crackers** taste good together.

count

You count things to find out how many of them you have.

Stand still so that I can **count** you all!

cowboy

A cowboy is someone who rides a horse and looks after the cattle on a big farm.

Woody is the best **cowboy** in the whole world!

crocodile

A crocodile is an animal with short legs, thick skin and a long snout. Crocodiles live in salty water.

That **crocodile** has a lot of teeth to brush!

cousin

Your cousin is the child of your aunt and uncle.

If Aunt Flora had a daughter, she would be Aurora's **cousin**.

crab

A crab is an animal with a hard shell that lives in the sea. It has eight legs and two big claws.

Sebastian the **crab** tries to keep Ariel out of trouble.

cross

When you cross something, you go from one side to the other.

The road is too busy for Lady to **cross**.

crown

A crown is a round object made of gold and jewels. Kings and queens wear a crown on their head.

Robin Hood thought the best thing about King John was his **crown**.

cup

A cup is a container with a handle. You drink from a cup.

Would you like a **cup** of tea?

cut

When you cut something, you use a knife or a pair of scissors to divide it into parts.

Gus and Jaq **cut** a long piece of ribbon for Cinderella's dress.

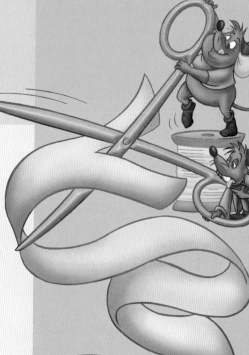

cry

When you cry, tears fall from your eyes because you are sad or angry.

Daisy starts to **cry** when she watches a sad film.

cupboard

A cupboard is a piece of furniture with doors and shelves. You keep things in a cupboard.

All the dishes were put away in the **cupboard**.

cucumber

A cucumber is a long thin vegetable with a green skin. You usually eat cucumber raw in salads.

The best way to eat a **cucumber** is in slices.

cushion

A cushion is a cloth bag with soft material inside it. You put cushions on a chair or a sofa.

The **cushions** on the sofa are so soft!

cymbal

A cymbal is a big circle of metal. You bang two cymbals together to make a loud musical sound.

Crash! The Scat Cat Band loves to play the **cymbals**.

Dd

dog

a b c **d** e f g h i j k l m n o p q r s t u v w x y z

dancer

A dancer is someone who likes to move to music.

Donald is a surprisingly graceful **dancer**.

deer

A deer is an animal with four legs that lives in the forest. Young deer have spots on their fur.

This young **deer** is the Prince of the Forest, Bambi!

daughter

A daughter is a female child.

Mulan is the **daughter** in her family.

dentist

A dentist helps to look after your teeth.

This **dentist** uses a lot of tools to clean teeth!

dance

When you dance, you move your body to music.

Belle and the Beast **dance** together beautifully.

day

A day is 24 hours long. The morning, the afternoon and the evening are all part of one day.

My favourite **day** is Saturday!

department store

A department store is a big shop that sells many different things.

There are so many different things to buy in this **department store**.

desert

A desert is a very dry place. Many deserts are hot and sandy.

Aladdin doesn't like being in the **desert**, but his friend does!

dinner

Dinner is the main meal of the day.

Who invited them to **dinner**?

desk

A desk is a piece of furniture that you sit behind. You write and do other kinds of work at a desk.

You will do a lot of work at your **desk** at school.

different

If something is different, it is not like other things.

Ariel is **different** from her sisters.

dinosaur

A dinosaur is a large animal that lived millions of years ago. There are no dinosaurs alive now.

This **dinosaur** doesn't look very fierce!

dessert

A dessert is a sweet food that you eat at the end of a meal.

Grab a spoon and dig into this delicious **dessert**.

difficult

If something is difficult, it is hard to do or to understand.

Minnie has just learned to play a very **difficult** piece of music.

direction

A direction is somewhere you look at or point to.

Is Geppetto in this **direction**?

dirty

When something is dirty, it is not clean.

It's fun to get **dirty**!

dishwasher

A dishwasher is a machine that washes things such as plates, cups, glasses, knives and forks.

The **dishwasher** makes dirty plates clean and shiny!

dog

A dog is a pet that barks and wags its tail when it's happy.

Lady and Tramp are two **dogs** in love.

disagree

If you disagree with somebody, you each have different ideas about something.

I **disagree**! Baseball is more fun than chess.

do

When you do something, you make it happen.

Cinderella has a lot of sewing to **do**.

doll

A doll is a toy that looks like a person.

A **doll** is always ready to be your friend!

dish

A dish is a container for holding food.

You can find **dishes** in lots of different sizes and colours.

doctor

A doctor helps to make you feel better when you are ill.

This monster is pretending to be a **doctor**.

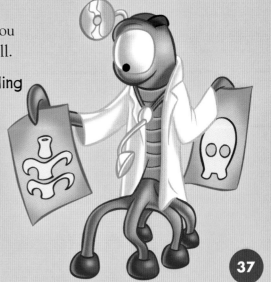

a b c **d** e f g h i j k l m n o p q r s t u v w x y z

dolphin

A dolphin is a very clever creature that lives in the sea. Dolphins are friendly and they like to swim with people.

Would you like to swim with a **dolphin**?

drawer

A drawer is part of a piece of furniture. It slides in and out and holds things.

You can keep your pyjamas in one **drawer**, and your shirts in another.

door

You open and close a door to get in and out of a room or a building.

What do you think is behind that **door**?

down

When something goes down, it moves to a lower place.

Be very careful coming **down** the stairs!

dream

When you dream you make up stories while you are asleep.

Donald **dreams** that Daisy is having a good time at the seaside.

doorbell

A doorbell is outside a house. When you press it, it rings to let people know you are there.

Brrring! Ring the **doorbell** again to make sure Minnie knows we're here!

MiNNiE

draw

When you draw, you make pictures with a pencil, a pen, a crayon or chalk.

Jane loves to **draw** everything in the jungle.

dress

A dress is a top and a skirt that are joined together as one piece. Girls and women wear dresses.

Do you like my pink **dress**?

drive

When you are old enough to drive, you can steer a vehicle such as a car or a lorry.

Would you like to **drive** a taxi in Monstropolis?

driver

A driver is someone who drives.

Do you think Donald is a good **driver**?

drum

A drum is a round musical instrument. You bang on it with sticks to make a sound.

The Scat Cat Band can really play those **drums**!

dry

When something is dry, it is not wet.

Ha! Do you think you'll ever get **dry**?!

drink

A drink is a liquid food such as milk or water.

Pluto has a **drink** of water on a hot afternoon.

drop

When you drop something, you let it fall.

Be careful you don't **drop** your ice cream on the ground!

duck

A duck is a flying bird that quacks. Ducks like to live and swim in water.

Ducks don't like to be chased by dogs!

a b c **d** e f g h i j k l m n o p q r s t u v w x y z

a b c d **e** f g h i j k l m n o p q r s t u v w x y z

elephant

earth

Earth is the name of the planet that you live on.

Planet **Earth** is out here somewhere!

eat

When you eat, you take food into your mouth, chew it and then swallow it.

I can **eat** a lot of these!

east

East is the opposite direction of west.

The sun rises in the **east** each morning.

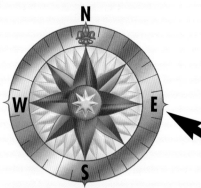

egg

An egg is a round or oval object with a shell. Some baby animals grow inside an egg until they are ready to be born.

All female birds lay **eggs**.

E e

early

Early means before the usual time.

Daisy is too **early** to buy her train ticket.

easy

If something is easy to do, it means it is not hard to do.

It's **easy** for Pluto to sing along to Goofy's music.

elbow

Your elbow is the middle part of your arm where it bends.

Pinocchio is bending his right **elbow**!

empty

Empty means that there is nothing inside.

Garsh! This is **empty** except for my socks!

entrance

An entrance is the opening you walk through to go inside a building.

Mickey goes through the **entrance** to meet Minnie.

elephant

An elephant is a large animal with big ears, and a long nose called a trunk.

An **elephant** lifts up its trunk when it's happy.

engine

An engine is a machine that makes things move.

This **engine** is from a big aeroplane.

envelope

An envelope is what you send a letter in.

You need a stamp on your **envelope** before you can post it.

e-mail

An e-mail is the kind of letter that you receive through your computer.

Lilo sends an **e-mail** every day to her Elvis Fan Club.

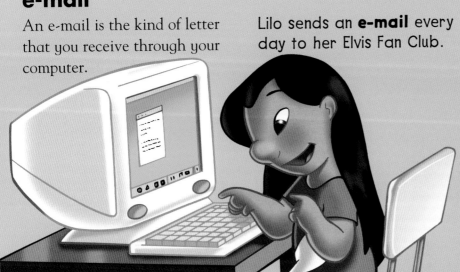

escalator

An escalator is a moving staircase that takes you up or down from one floor to the next.

Oh, no! This **escalator** leads to even more shops.

41

a b c d **e** f g h i j k l m n o p q r s t u v w x y z

evening

Evening is the early part of the night. It starts with the sunset.

This **evening** is going to be fun!

exciting

Something is exciting when it feels good to think about it or do it.

We're on an **exciting** magic carpet ride!

everyone

Everyone means everybody.

Everyone plays tug-of-war with the cushion!

exit

An exit is the opening you walk through to leave a building.

Goofy walks through the **exit** to the roof garden.

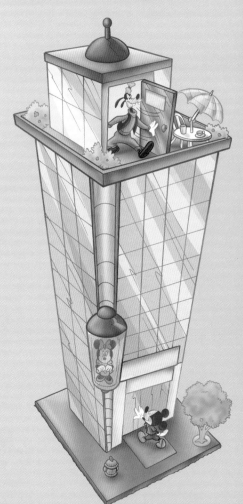

everything

Everything means all things.

It's **everything** I could ever want!

excited

You feel excited when you are waiting for, or doing, something that makes you happy.

Andy is **excited** about opening his birthday present.

a b c d **e** f g h i j k l m n o p q r s t u v w x y z

42

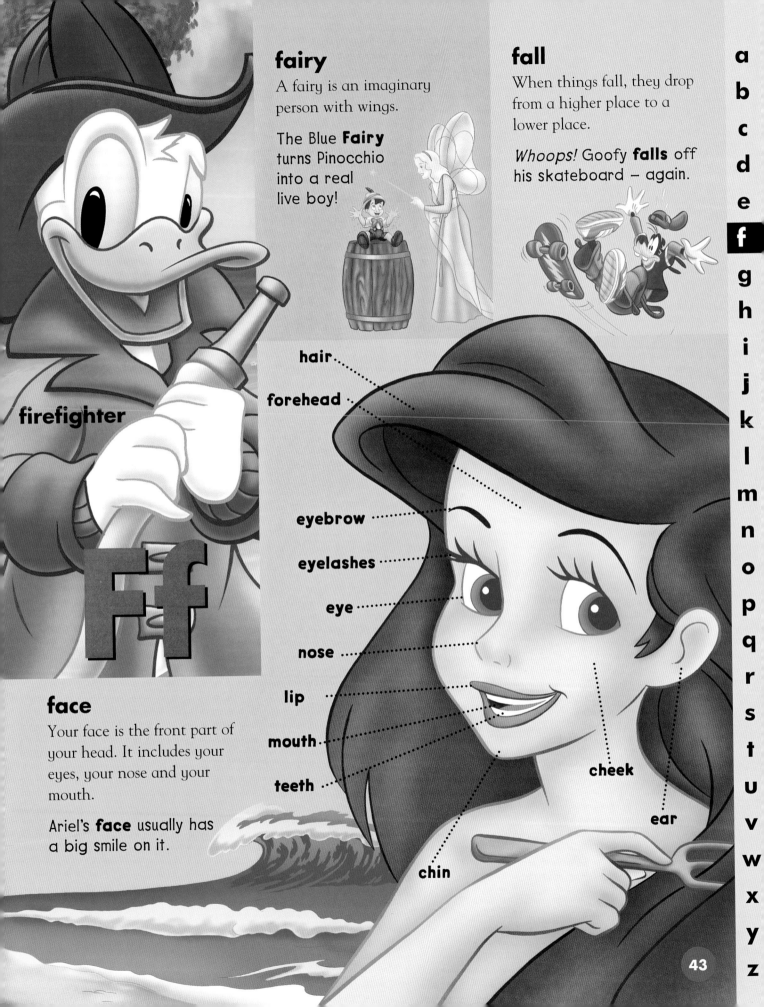

fairy

A fairy is an imaginary person with wings.

The Blue **Fairy** turns Pinocchio into a real live boy!

fall

When things fall, they drop from a higher place to a lower place.

Whoops! Goofy **falls** off his skateboard – again.

firefighter

Ff

face

Your face is the front part of your head. It includes your eyes, your nose and your mouth.

Ariel's **face** usually has a big smile on it.

hair

forehead

eyebrow

eyelashes

eye

nose

lip

mouth

teeth

cheek

ear

chin

a b c d e **f** g h i j k l m n o p q r s t u v w x y z

fan

A fan is a machine that moves air around to make you feel cooler.

Ahhh! That **fan** is such a good thing on a hot day.

fast

When something is fast, it happens quickly.

Abu runs as **fast** as he can!

far

If something is far from you, it is a long way away.

Simba is **far** ahead of Nala.

father

Your father is your male parent.

I'll always be your **father**, Simba.

feather

A feather is a part of a bird that helps it to fly and to keep warm. Birds have lots of feathers.

This bird's **feathers** are fluffy and white.

farmer

A farmer is someone who works on a farm.

That **farmer** has only planted one thing – himself!

feel

When you feel something, you touch it or it touches you in a certain way.

Lady's fur **feels** so soft!

fence

A fence is a kind of wall between two places.

This **fence** is between Donald's garden and his neighbour's garden.

fight

A fight is an argument when one person tries to hurt another person.

Anastasia and Drizella are having another **fight** about Prince Charming.

fire

A fire is the heat, the flames and the light that happen when something burns.

Cowboys use an outdoor **fire** to cook their supper.

fever

A fever is extra heat in the body of an ill person.

The thermometer shows that Wendy Darling has a **fever**.

finish

To finish something is to come to the end of it.

Simba and Nala are about to **finish** their race.

firefighter

A firefighter is a person whose job it is to put out fires.

I'm proud to be a **firefighter**!

field

A field is a flat, open piece of land with no buildings in it. A farmer grows crops or keeps animals in a field.

Bambi and Faline play in the **field** of flowers.

fireplace

A fireplace is an area where adults can make a safe fire to warm up a room.

A **fireplace** makes the room feel cosy.

a b c d e **f** g h i j k l m n o p q r s t u v w x y z

a b c d e f g h i j k l m n o p q r s t u v w x y z

firework

When it is lit, a firework makes a loud noise and beautiful, bright lights in the sky.

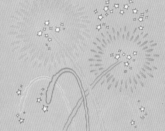

Fireworks are so colourful – and so loud!

fish

A fish is an animal with fins that lives in the water. Fish breathe through parts called gills.

Hi! I'm Flounder the **fish**, and the Little Mermaid is my best friend!

first

When something comes first, it comes before everything else.

Doc is the **first** in the line of Dwarfs.

fish bowl

A fish bowl is a see-through container that holds water and pet fish.

The fish can see lots from their **fish bowl**.

flag

A flag is a piece of cloth with a coloured design on it that stands for something.

What shape can you see in the centre of this **flag**?

first-aid kit

A first-aid kit is a container that holds things to treat an injury or illness.

It's a good idea to keep a **first-aid kit** in your home.

fishing rod

A fishing rod is a long thin pole. You use a fishing rod to catch fish.

You might need to use both hands to hold a **fishing rod**.

float

To float means to stay on top of the water and not sink.

This is the only way to **float**, Stitch!

46

floor

A floor is the part of a room that you walk on.

Be careful! The **floor** is slippery.

flower

A flower is the colourful part of a plant. It has petals and contains the plant's seeds.

Flowers come in so many bright colours!

fly

A fly is an insect with two clear wings.

That **fly** is buzzing about, looking for food.

florist

A florist is a person who sells flowers.

You can buy all sorts of pretty flowers from a **florist**.

flute

A flute is a musical instrument that is shaped like a long tube. You hold a flute sideways and play by blowing into a hole.

A **flute** can make high sounds.

fold

When you fold something, you bend one part of it over the other.

Huey and Dewey **fold** the paper from their notebooks, and suddenly homework is more fun!

flour

Flour is a white or brown powder that you use to bake bread and cakes.

We need two scoops of **flour** from the sack for our cake.

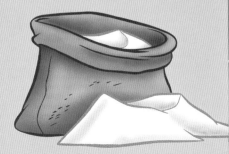

fly

To fly means to move through the air.

Zazu tries to **fly** out of Simba's reach.

follow

When you follow something, you go after it or behind it.

Follow me if you want a big adventure!

fork

You use a fork when you eat your food. It has long pointed parts and a handle.

You can use a **fork** to pick up your food.

free

If something is free it does not cost anything.

Pinocchio, do you think these sweets are **free**?

footprint

A footprint is the mark that a foot or a shoe makes.

The lion's paws make big **footprints** in the sand.

fountain

A fountain is a jet of water that shoots up into the air. The water comes down in pretty streams.

This **fountain** is in the middle of a park.

freeze

Water freezes when it gets so cold that it turns into ice.

Brrr! The water on Mushu's tail is starting to **freeze**!

forget

When you forget something, you cannot remember it.

How could Donald **forget** his money?

fox

A fox is an animal with red fur, a pointed nose and a bushy tail. Foxes live in forests.

This **fox** is good at keeping out of trouble!

fresh

If a food is fresh it has just been picked or made.

I love to eat **fresh** vegetables from our garden.

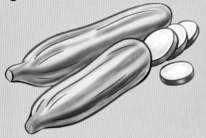

front

The front of something is the part that faces forwards. The front is the opposite side to the back.

There is a big sign on the **front** of Pluto's kennel.

fur

Fur is the thick hair on the bodies of many animals.

Fur comes in many colours, such as grey, white and brown.

friend

A friend is someone you like and have fun with.

Woody is my best **friend**.

frown

A frown is the look on the face of a worried person. If you frown, the ends of your mouth turn down.

Don't **frown** at the camera, Stitch!

furniture

Furniture is the objects that you have in your house, such as tables, chairs, cupboards and beds.

Where should Mickey put this piece of **furniture**?

frog

A frog is a small hopping animal with a smooth skin. It makes a croaking noise that sounds like "ribbit".

This **frog** lives in a pond.

full

Full means that there is no room for anything else.

Minnie's refrigerator is completely **full**!

a
b
c
d
e
f
g
h
i
j
k
l
m
n
o
p
q
r
s
t
u
v
w
x
y
z

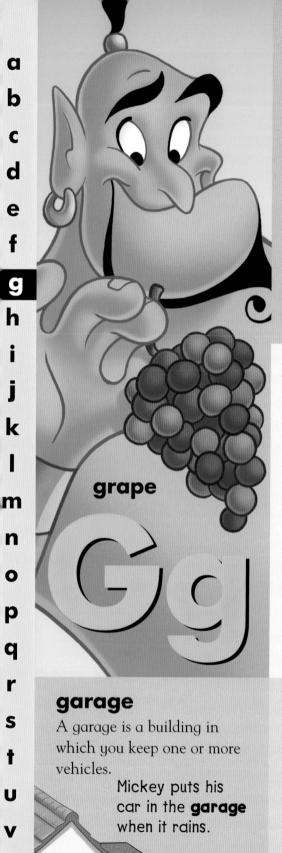

a b c d e f **g** h i j k l m n o p q r s t u v w x y z

garden

A garden is a place where people grow flowers, vegetables and other plants.

> I water my **garden** to help the plants grow!

grape

Gg

generous

If someone is generous, that person is kind and gives money and things to others.

Robin Hood is a very **generous** person.

get

To get something is to borrow, buy or receive it from someone else.

Pluto **gets** a special present!

garage

A garage is a building in which you keep one or more vehicles.

Mickey puts his car in the **garage** when it rains.

genie

A genie is a make-believe person who usually lives in a magic lamp. Genies can make wishes come true.

> Hiya, Al! Your personal **genie** here, at your service.

ghost

People think that a ghost is the spirit of someone who has died.

A friendly **ghost** might say "boo" to scare you.

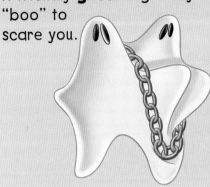

girl

A girl is a child who will grow up to become a woman.

Aloha! I'm a **girl** called Lilo. Who are you?

glasses

Glasses have a frame with special glass in them. You wear glasses in front of your eyes to help you see better.

When you are older you may need to wear **glasses**.

giraffe

A giraffe is a very tall animal with long thin legs and a very long neck.

Because of its long neck, a **giraffe** can reach the leaves on the tallest trees.

give

When you give to someone, you let the person have something.

Roly, **give** the remote control to Roger! It's time to watch television.

glass

A glass is a container that you drink from.

This **glass** is half full.

globe

A globe is a round map of the world.

A **globe** can show you all the water and all the land on the Earth.

a
b
c
d
e
f
g
h
i
j
k
l
m
n
o
p
q
r
t
u
v
w
x
y
z

a b c d e f g h i j k l m n o p q r s t u v w x y z

glove

A glove is a piece of clothing that covers each finger separately. Gloves keep your hands warm or clean.

You can wiggle your fingers inside your **gloves**!

goal

In some sports, a goal is the place where you try to put the ball to score points.

Hooray! Donald kicked the ball into the **goal**!

glue

Glue is a sticky liquid that lets you join one thing onto another.

The **glue** will drip if you leave the top off the tube!

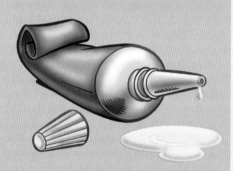

goldfish

A goldfish is a small orange fish that you can keep as a pet.

The **goldfish** jumps with happiness because of its new home.

good

Someone that you like or something that is done well is good.

Abu is one of Aladdin's **good** friends.

go

To go means to move from one place to another.

Tarzan can **go** through the jungle without touching the ground!

gorilla

A gorilla is a large and strong wild animal that comes from Africa.

This **gorilla** bangs on its chest to tell everyone it's here.

52

grandchild

When you grow up, the child of your son or your daughter will be your grandchild.

Huey, Dewey and Louie are Grandma Duck's **grandchildren**.

grapefruit

A grapefruit is a big, round juicy fruit that grows on a tree.

This **grapefruit** is yellow, but some are pink.

greengrocer

A greengrocer is someone who sells fruits and vegetables in a shop.

What would you like to buy from this **greengrocer**?

grandparent

Your grandparent is the parent of your mother or your father.

Mulan's favourite **grandparent** is her Grandmother Fa.

grape

A grape is a small round fruit that grows in bunches on a vine.

Do you like to eat **grapes**?

guess

When you guess something, you say what you think is right, but you aren't sure if it's the right answer.

Guess what's behind my back!

grass

Grass is a plant that grows in parks, gardens and fields.

The **grass** at the edge of the field is very tall.

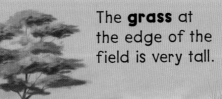

guitar

A guitar is a big musical instrument. You play a guitar by plucking its strings.

Most of the Scat Cat Band members can play the **guitar**.

a b c d e f **g** h i j k l m n o p q r s t u v w x y z

hat

Hh

hairdresser

A hairdresser is a person who cuts and styles someone's hair.

A good hairdresser uses all his hands at once!

ham

Ham is a kind of smoked meat.

Ham and fresh vegetables make a delicious dinner.

hairdryer

A hairdryer is a machine that uses hot air to dry your hair.

With this hairdryer you can dry your wet hair quickly.

hamburger

A hamburger is made from minced meat, which is shaped into a flat circle and then cooked.

What do you like on your hamburger?

hairbrush

A hairbrush is a brush that you use to make your hair tidy.

You can use a hairbrush to make your hair look smart.

half

When you divide something into two equal parts, each part is one half of what you started with.

Which half of the pizza would you like to eat?

hammer

A hammer is a tool that you use to hit a nail into a piece of wood.

A carpenter always uses a hammer on the job.

handsome

A good-looking man is handsome.

Belle is in love with her **handsome** prince.

hard

Something is hard if it doesn't bend or change shape easily.

Call me Grumpy, but this bench is **hard**!

hang

When you hang something, you attach it at the top to something else.

After a hard day's work, the Dwarfs **hang** up their hats.

harmonica

A harmonica is a musical instrument with rows of tiny square holes that you blow into.

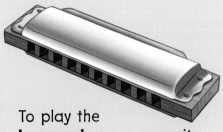

To play the **harmonica** you move it backwards and forwards in front of your mouth.

hat

A hat is a piece of clothing that you wear on your head.

Perla has a brand-new **hat** for spring.

happy

You are happy when you feel good about something.

Happy got his name because he's always **happy**!

harp

A harp is a large heavy musical instrument. You lean against a harp while you pluck its strings.

Duchess makes beautiful music on the **harp**.

hate

When you hate something, you really don't like it at all.

That crocodile really **hates** Captain Hook!

a b c d e f g **h** i j k l m n o p q r s t u v w x y z

have

When you have something, it is with you, it is part of you or it belongs to you.

Snow White shouldn't **have** that apple!

heavy

When something is heavy it is difficult to lift.

The small box is very **heavy**.

healthy

To be healthy means to feel well.

Running helps keep me **healthy**.

helicopter

A helicopter is a flying machine with spinning blades on the top.

You can see a lot of things below you when you fly in a **helicopter**.

hen

A hen is a female chicken.

This **hen** lives on a farm with her two baby chicks.

hear

When you hear something, it means you listen to the sounds that reach your ears.

Thomas O'Malley likes to **hear** good music.

help

When you help someone, you do something to make things easier for that person.

I'll **help** you to reach the food!

here

Here means in this place.

So many books! I think I like it **here**.

hide

To hide means to put something in a place where it cannot be easily found.

*I'm going to **hide** under this cone!*

hip

Your hip is the part of your body between your waist and the top of your leg.

Pinocchio places his hand on his right **hip**.

hold

To hold something is to keep it in place.

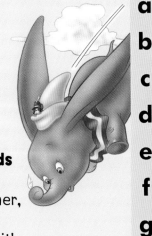

Dumbo **holds** on tightly to his feather, but he can fly without it!

high

Something that is high is far above something else.

Puppies love to jump up **high,** especially for a treat.

hippopotamus

A hippopotamus is an African animal with a large body and short legs. It spends a lot of time in water.

A **hippopotamus** can move around more easily in the water than on land.

hole

A hole is an open space in something.

Gaston's big toe peeps out of the **hole** in his sock.

hit

When you hit something, you strike it hard with something such as your hand.

Oops! Louie didn't mean to **hit** Uncle Donald!

holiday

A holiday is a special day when you celebrate something important.

Belle and the Beast enjoy spending every **holiday** together.

a b c d e f g **h** i j k l m n o p q r s t u v w x y z

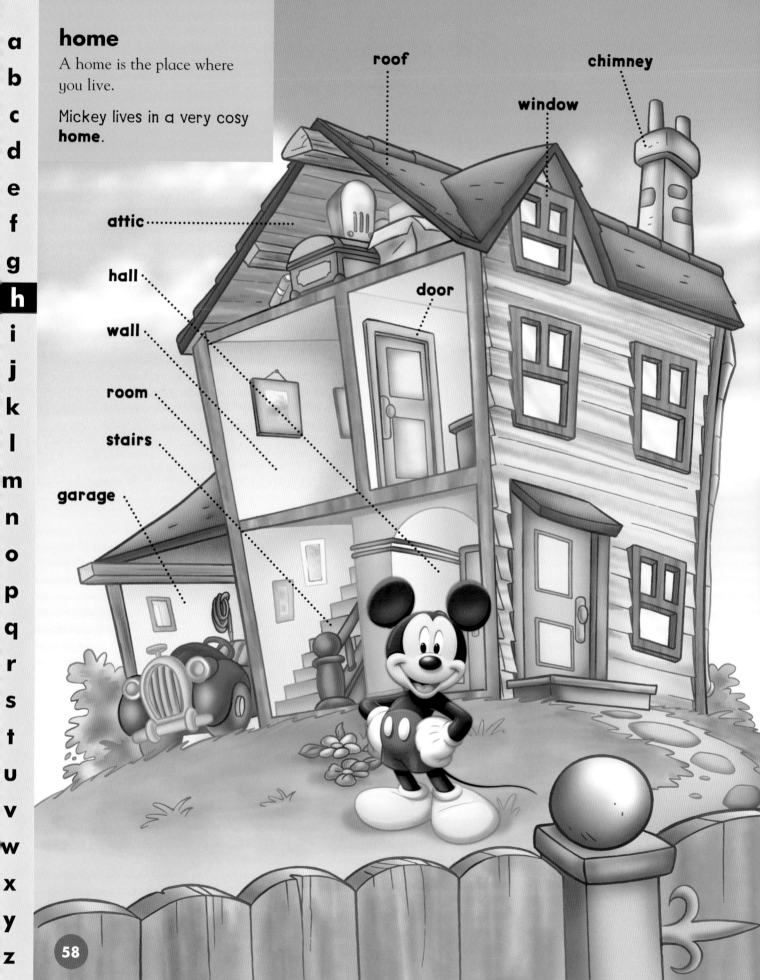

a b c d e f g **h** i j k l m n o p q r s t u v w x y z

home

A home is the place where you live.

Mickey lives in a very cosy **home**.

roof

chimney

window

attic

door

hall

wall

room

stairs

garage

58

homework

Homework is the schoolwork that you do at home.

Sometimes the **homework** is difficult!

hope

When you hope for something, you wish for it.

Geppetto **hopes** to have a son.

honey

Honey is a sticky sweet syrup that is made by bees.

Honey tastes delicious on bread.

horse

A horse is a large animal with long legs and a long tail. It has thick hair on its neck called a mane.

A **horse** can run very fast.

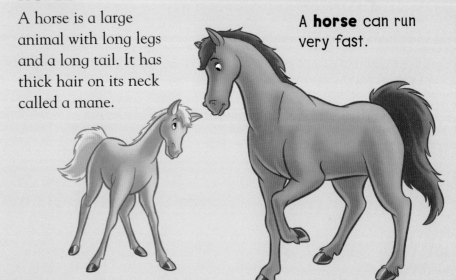

hop

To hop is to jump.

Hop across to the other side, Bambi. You can do it!

hospital

A hospital is a place where people go when they are ill and need special care to get better.

A lot of doctors and nurses work in a **hospital**.

a b c d e f g **h** i j k l m n o p q r s t u v w x y z

59

hot

If something is hot it is very warm.

The Genie likes hot summer days.

hot dog

A hot dog is a long thin sausage inside a bread roll. You often eat a hot dog with ketchup on it.

A hot dog is Huey's favourite food!

hotel

A hotel is a big building with lots of bedrooms. People sleep in a hotel when they are travelling.

This hotel is in the middle of a busy city.

hour

An hour is a period of time, made up of 60 minutes. There are 24 hours in a day.

Sulley arrives for work at the start of the hour.

hug

When you hug someone, you put your arms around them.

Kala hugs her son Tarzan.

hungry

When you are hungry, you want something to eat.

Dopey is very hungry!

hurry

When you hurry, you move quickly because you want to get somewhere fast.

If we hurry and catch that lorry it will take us back home!

husband

A husband is a man who is married to a woman. She is called his wife.

Roger is Anita's husband.

ice cream

ice cream

Ice cream is a frozen food made of milk or cream, sugar and flavourings such as chocolate or vanilla.

Mmmm! It's easy to finish **ice cream** before it melts!

ice skate

An ice skate is a high shoe with a blade on the bottom. You wear ice skates to skate on ice.

These **ice skates** fit us perfectly!

idea

An idea is a thought that you have about something.

I have an **idea** how to rescue Woody!

in

In means within or surrounded by.

Simba is **in** the cave.

ice

Ice is frozen water.

The **ice** is very slippery, isn't it, Bambi?

a b c d e f g h **i** j k l m n o p q r s t u v w x y z

insect

An insect is a small animal with six legs. Some insects have two pairs of wings.

There are more **insects** in the world than any other animal.

invite

When you invite people to visit or do something with you, you let them know you want them to join you.

Ariel is going to **invite** her friends to an under-the-sea concert.

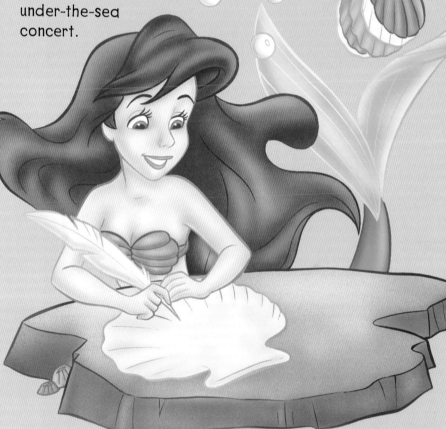

interesting

When something is interesting you want to know more about it.

Buzz thinks this rocket is so **interesting** that he wants to know how it works.

iron

An iron is a metal object with a flat metal bottom that you heat up. You use an iron to smoothe out the wrinkles in clothes.

Nani will have to use the **iron** on Lilo's shirt again.

island

An island is a piece of land that is surrounded by water.

This **island** has a very tall mountain.

jacket

Jj

jam

Jam is a sweet food that is made from fruit and sugar. You can spread jam on a slice of bread.

What kind of jam do you like?

jewellery

Jewellery describes things such as rings, bracelets and necklaces. People wear jewellery to decorate themselves.

Look at Jasmine's pretty **jewellery**.

jar

A jar is a glass container with a lid. You keep food and other things in a jar.

This jar will keep food fresh.

jigsaw

A jigsaw is a picture puzzle made of wooden or cardboard pieces. You put the pieces together to make the picture.

Whose face is on this jigsaw?

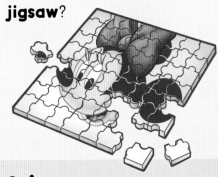

jacket

A jacket is a short coat.

This jacket has a zip.

jeans

Jeans are trousers that are made from a material called denim.

Jeans are strong enough to wear in the playground.

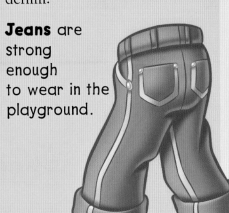

juice

Juice is the liquid that comes from fruit or vegetables when you squeeze them.

Apple **juice** is a drink made from apples.

a
b
c
d
e
f
g
h
i
j
k
l
m
n
o
p
q
r
s
t
u
v
w
x
y
z

juggle

To juggle is to throw things high into the air and then catch them, one at a time.

Do you think you could **juggle** like this?

jump

When you jump, you push yourself off the ground with both feet.

The Beast lands on his feet after he **jumps**.

jungle

A jungle is a hot place that is filled with trees, flowers and wild animals.

Kerchak the gorilla is the king of the **jungle**.

kiss

Kk

keep

When you keep something, you hold on to it.

Lilo plans to **keep** Stitch forever.

kick

When you kick, you make a strong, forceful movement with your foot or feet.

Ariel is so happy to have legs that she **kicks** them up in the air!

key

A key is a metal object that opens a lock.

This **key** fits into a special lock.

king

A king is the ruler of a country.

King Stefan is Sleeping Beauty's father.

kangaroo

A kangaroo is an animal with big feet that jumps. A mother kangaroo carries her baby in a pouch in her tummy.

Kangaroos come from Australia.

keyboard

A keyboard is the long row of keys on a piano or a computer.

A piano **keyboard** has 88 keys.

kiss

A kiss is a touch you make with your lips.

Bo Peep gives Woody a **kiss** on his cheek.

a b c d e f g h i j **k** l m n o p q r s t u v w x y

kitchen

A kitchen is the room in your home where you prepare food.

Lilo and Stitch have to clean up this **kitchen**!

knife

A knife is a tool for cutting things and for spreading.

You use a **knife** like this to spread butter on your toast.

knock

When you knock on something, you hit it to make a sound.

Snow White **knocks** on the door of the Dwarfs' cottage.

kite

A kite is a toy that flies in the wind. It is made of wood, paper and string.

Look how high in the sky that **kite** is flying!

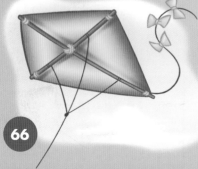

kitten

A kitten is a very young cat.

This **kitten** is *sooo* sweet!

know

When you know something, you have learned about it and can remember it.

I **know** that I must always go to school!

lion

lamp

A lamp gives off light and usually works by electricity.

You turn on a **lamp** when the room gets dark.

late

Late means after the time that something is supposed to happen.

I'm **late** for a very important date!

large

Large is another word for big.

Gus is a **large** mouse.

later

Later means at another time, but not now.

Robin Hood will give the money to the poor **later**.

ladder

A ladder is a long set of steps you can move around. You climb up a ladder to reach something high.

Each step of a **ladder** is called a rung.

last

The last one is the one that comes after all the others.

Dopey is the **last** Dwarf in the line. The turtle is the very **last** creature of all.

a b c d e f g h i j k **l** m n o p q r s t u v w x y z

laugh

When you laugh, you make a special sound that means you find something funny.

Belle and the Beast **laugh** together.

learn

When you learn something, you find out about new things.

You **learn** something new in school every day.

lazy

When you feel lazy, it means that you don't feel like doing anything.

Donald is so **lazy**!

least

The least of something is the smallest part of it.

Baking cakes is the **least** of Donald's talents.

left

Left is the opposite of right.

Simba is on the **left** side of the tree.

leaf

A leaf is the flat part of a plant that grows on the stem or branch.

This **leaf** fell from a tree in the autumn.

leave

When you leave something, you go away from it.

Mike will **leave** his lunch box in the locker.

lemon

A lemon is a sour yellow fruit that grows on a tree.

You can make sweet lemonade with **lemons** – if you add lots of sugar!

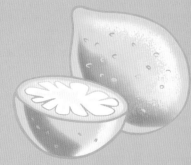

less

Less means not as much as something else.

It takes Donald **less** time to fry an egg than to make a sandwich.

lesson

A lesson is something you learn, which you didn't know before.

The monsters have a new **lesson** in scaring each week.

lettuce

Lettuce is a green vegetable with large leaves. You often eat lettuce as salad.

There are many different kinds of **lettuce**, such as iceberg and romaine.

library

A library is a building with a lot of books that you can borrow.

The **library** has many books that you can take home to read!

lie

When someone lies, that person is saying something that is not true.

Pinocchio, don't **lie** to me. Tell me the truth. What happened?

lifeguard

A lifeguard is a person who works at the beach, to make sure that people swim safely.

A **lifeguard** must be a strong swimmer.

lift

To lift something means to pick it up.

Come on, Goofy – you can **lift** the suitcase. Pull!

light

A light is a kind of brightness.

Tinker Bell's **light** glows wherever she goes.

a b c d e f g h i j k **l** m n o p q r s t u v w x y z

light

If something is light, it doesn't weigh very much at all.

The big box is **light** because it is full of feathers.

line

A line is a long thin mark or a row of something.

The women who wanted to dance with the Prince stood in a long **line**.

lightning

Lightning is the flash of light that you see in the sky just before you hear thunder.

When it rained last night, there was a big flash of **lightning** in the sky.

lion

A lion is a large wild cat that roars. The male lion has a mane of fur around his neck.

I'm Simba, and I've just become the **Lion** King!

live

To live means to be alive.

Donald **lives** the good life!

like

If you like something or someone, you feel good about them.

Meeko really **likes** those biscuits!

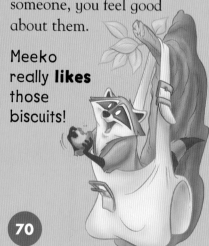

listen

When you listen to something or someone, you pay attention.

Listen to me, Pinocchio! I can help you.

living room

A living room is the room in a home where people spend a lot of time together.

Pluto watches his favourite video in Mickey's **living room**.

long

When something is long, the beginning is far away from the end.

In the top picture, Mulan's hair is **long**.

lose

If you lose a game or a race you do not win it.

Pumbaa **loses** every race against Timon!

low

Something that is low is close to the ground.

Hooray! The bone is **low** enough to reach now!

look

When you look at something or someone, you pay attention to what you are seeing.

Mowgli **looks** at Kaa, and the snake puts a spell on him!

lost

You are lost if you don't know where you are.

I can't be **lost**! The map must be wrong.

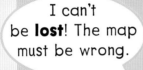

lunch

Lunch is the second meal of the day.

Donald needs a good **lunch** to get some more energy!

lorry

A lorry is a big road vehicle that carries heavy loads.

This **lorry** has big wheels at the front and smaller ones at the back.

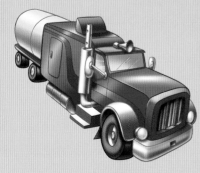

love

To love someone or something means that you care a lot.

Sulley and his friend Boo **love** each other very much.

monster

Mm

magazine

A magazine is a soft-covered book with news, stories and pictures inside it.

There seems to be a **magazine** for every interest.

magic

Magic is the power to make impossible things happen, with the help of charms or spells.

A little **magic** makes the housework easier!

magician

A magician is someone who performs magic.

This **magician** can do lots of tricks!

make

When you make something, you create it, put it together or change one thing into something else.

I can **make** a lot of things out of wood.

machine

A machine is something that is built to do or make things.

Maurice's new **machine** is ready for testing.

man

A boy grows up to become a man.

Mr Darling is the **man** of the family.

map

A map is a picture that shows you where places and things are.

This map shows the United States of America.

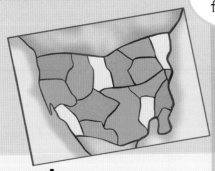

me

Me is another way, apart from "I", of referring to yourself.

Can you find **me**?

mean

Someone who is mean is unkind to others.

The Cheshire Cat annoys Alice, but he isn't really **mean** to her.

match

When two things match, they are the same.

Tweedledee and Tweedledum **match** each other perfectly!

meal

A meal is the food you eat at one time. You have three meals a day: breakfast, lunch and dinner.

Wow! I'm having three **meals** in one go!

measure

When you measure something, you find out how tall, wide or deep it is.

Jiminy Cricket **measures** Pinocchio's *lo-oo-ong* nose.

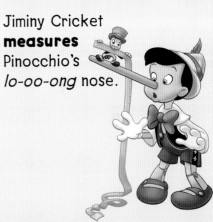

maths

When you learn maths, you find out about numbers.

I need to know **maths** to count all you Dalmatians!

meat

Meat is food such as chicken, lamb, beef, turkey or pork.

This roast meat is ready to serve.

a b c d e f g h i j k l **m** n o p q r s t u v w x y z

medicine

Medicine is something that you take when you are ill to help make you better.

The doctor might give you some **medicine** when you are ill.

melon

A melon is a large, ball-shaped fruit that is sweet and juicy inside.

A slice of fresh **melon** tastes good, even if it's messy to eat!

metal

Metal is a strong, hard material. Gold, silver and iron are different kinds of metal.

These pliers are made out of **metal**.

meet

When two people or things come together, they meet.

I am honoured to **meet** you, Princess Jasmine!

melt

To melt means to go from being solid or frozen to being liquid.

Thumper drinks the snow as it **melts**.

microphone

A microphone is a machine that helps to make sounds louder or to record them.

A singer uses a **microphone**.

mermaid

A mermaid is a girl or woman with human arms and a fishtail for legs. Mermaids live in the sea.

Welcome to my home under the sea. I'm Ariel, the Little **Mermaid**!

microwave oven

A microwave oven cooks food faster than an ordinary oven.

It looks as if Donald has been using the **microwave oven**!

milkshake

A milkshake is a thick, cold drink. It is made from milk, ice cream and a flavouring such as chocolate.

Slurp! It's fun to drink a **milkshake** through a straw!

miss

If you miss someone, you feel sad that you are not with him or her.

Ariel has started to **miss** Prince Eric.

midnight

Midnight is 12 o'clock at night.

A new day starts one second after **midnight**.

minute

A minute is made up of 60 seconds. There are 60 minutes in one hour.

It only took a **minute** for Alice to fall down the rabbit hole.

mistake

You make a mistake when you do something wrong.

Whoa! What a **mistake**! These flippers have got to go.

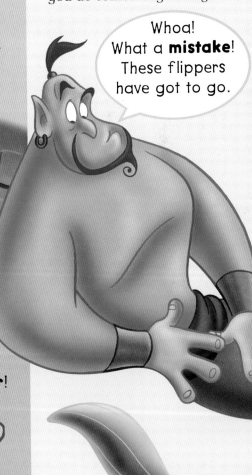

milk

Milk is a white liquid that you drink to make your bones strong.

Cats love fresh **milk**. Do you?

MILK

mirror

A mirror is a special type of glass in which you can see yourself.

Look who's in the **mirror**!

a b c d e f g h i j k l **m** n o p q r s t u v w x y z

a b c d e f g h i j k l **m** n o p q r s t u v w x y z

mix

When you mix things, you put them together to make something new.

Snow White is **mixing** up something delicious.

money

Money is the coins or notes that you use to buy things.

I have enough **money** for my big date with Celia!

monkey

A monkey is a furry animal with long legs and arms and usually a long tail.

A **monkey** likes to eat bananas.

monster

A monster is an imaginary creature that is a strange size, shape and colour.

This **monster** needs lots of gloves, socks and shoes!

moon

A moon is something that moves around a planet.

Our **moon** lights up the night sky.

more

More means a larger amount than something else.

Cinderella has lots **more** work to do.

morning

Morning is the early part of the day, before midday.

The Dwarfs go off to work every **morning**.

most

Most means the largest part of something.

Cinderella is the **most** beautiful girl at the ball.

mother

Your mother is your female parent.

In her heart, Kala is Tarzan's **mother**.

museum

A museum is a building that contains interesting things to look at and learn about.

This **museum** has Egyptian mummies on display!

mountain

A mountain is a very tall hill.

There's snow on the top of that **mountain**.

mouse

A mouse is the thing that you move around to make things happen on a computer.

You need to move the **mouse** to make it work.

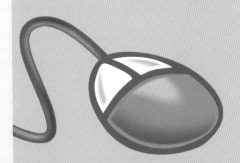

mushroom

A mushroom is a fungus that grows in dark, damp places.

Some **mushrooms** look like little umbrellas.

mouse

A mouse is a small grey or brown animal with long whiskers and a long tail. A mouse goes "squeak, squeak!"

I'm the only **mouse** who can do this!

moustache

A moustache is the hair that a man grows between his nose and his lips.

King Triton has a long **moustache** and beard.

musician

A musician is someone who plays an instrument.

This Scat Cat is a great **musician**!

a b c d e f g h i j k l **m** n o p q r s t u v w x y z

77

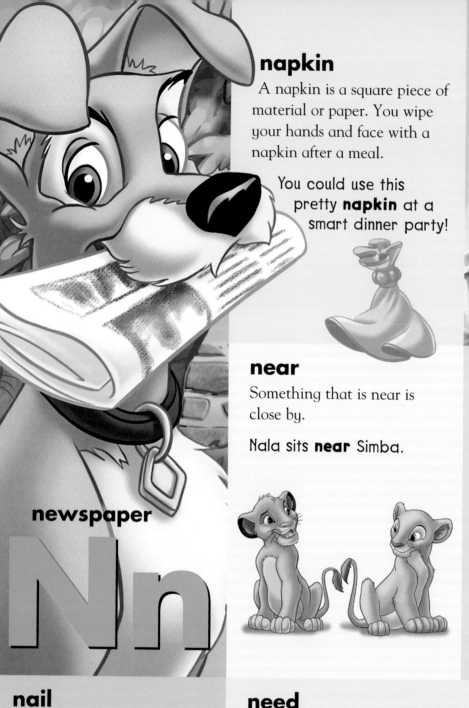

napkin

A napkin is a square piece of material or paper. You wipe your hands and face with a napkin after a meal.

You could use this pretty **napkin** at a smart dinner party!

neighbour

A neighbour is someone who lives very close to you.

Hi, **neighbour**! It's another beautiful day!

near

Something that is near is close by.

Nala sits **near** Simba.

nephew

Your nephew is the male child of your sister or brother.

Donald is glad that only one **nephew** came to visit today!

newspaper

Nn

nail

A nail is a thin piece of metal, with a point at one end. You hammer nails into wood to hold things together.

These **nails** can help Mickey build a new kennel for Pluto.

need

When you need something, you cannot do without it.

Mickey **needs** a towel!

nest

A nest is the home that birds and some other animals build for their babies.

How many baby birds can you count in this **nest**?

new

When something is new, it means that it has just been made or has never been used.

Daisy finds a good spot for her **new** vase.

nice

If someone or something is nice, you like that person or thing.

Sully thinks that Boo is **nice**.

net

A net is made of threads of rope or string. A net divides, stops, catches or holds things.

This **net** divides the tennis court into two halves.

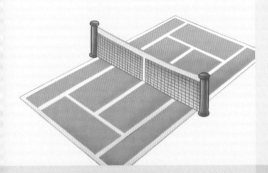

newspaper

A newspaper is big sheets of folded paper with all the news printed on them.

Tramp makes sure Jim Dear sees the **newspaper** straight away.

niece

A niece is the female child of your sister or brother.

Daisy has three **nieces** called April, May and June.

never

Never means not ever or at no time.

Snow White has **never** seen so many dirty plates!

next to

If you are next to someone, you are right beside that person.

I'm right **next to** you, Pumbaa, buddy!

a b c d e f g h i j k l m **n** o p q r s t u v w x y z

night

Night is the time between afternoon and morning.

Night is the best time to tell stories around a campfire.

noise

A noise is a kind of sound, often an unpleasant one.

This drum makes as much **noise** as a Genie – almost!

no

When someone says "no", that person does not believe something, does not want to do something or disagrees with something.

No! I can't go to the ball like this!

noon

Noon is 12 o'clock in the middle of the day.

It's **noon**. Time for lunch!

north

North is the opposite direction to south. On a map, something that is north of a place is above it.

If you keep travelling **north**, you will reach the North Pole – a very cold place.

no one

No one means not anyone at all.

No one wants to just rest on a cushion!

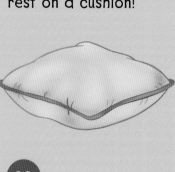

note

A note is a short message that you write.

Maid Marian finds a **note** from Robin Hood.

notebook

A notebook is a book with blank pages. You write things down in a notebook.

You can write your homework in this **notebook**.

nothing

Nothing means not anything at all.

Aladdin has a bunch of bananas, but Abu has **nothing**.

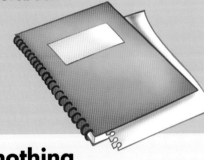

now

Now means at this time.

Simba is going to pounce – **now**!

number

A number is one of the units of maths that you use for counting.

Can you count the **numbers** one to ten? How high can you count?

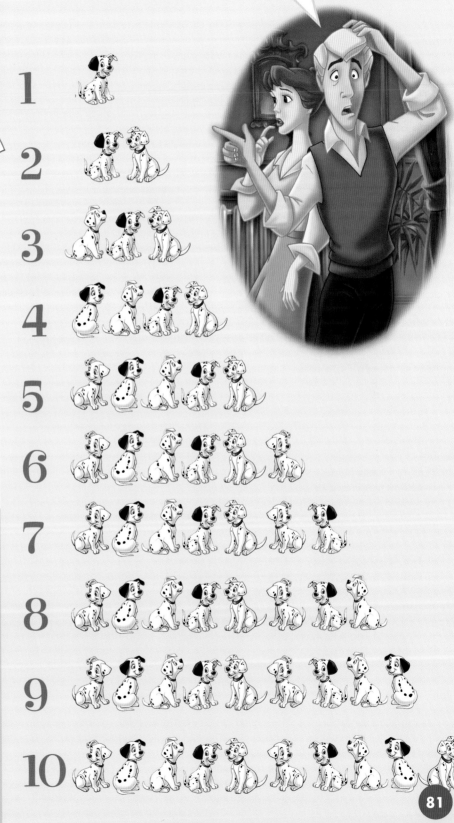

1

2

3

4

5

6

7

8

9

10

a b c d e f g h i j k l **m** n o p q r s t u v w x y z

oil

Oil is a thick, greasy liquid. You use some kinds of oil in machines, and other kinds are for cooking.

I use olive **oil** when I cook!

omelette

An omelette is a food made from fried eggs that are folded over. An omelette can hold a filling.

Do you like cheese in your **omelette**?

orange

old

Something or someone old has been around for a long time.

The younger monsters think Roz is **old**.

on

When someone is on something, that person is over and held up by the thing.

At last, I am **on** the throne!

octopus

An octopus is an animal with eight long arms that lives in the sea.

It takes a long time to shake hands with an **octopus**!

onion

An onion is a round vegetable with a strong taste and smell.

When you chop a fresh **onion** it might make your eyes water.

ostrich

An ostrich is a big bird with a long neck and long legs. Ostriches cannot fly, but they can run very fast.

The **ostrich** is the largest bird in the world.

over

Over can mean above, on top of or finished.

Watch me jump **over** you, Simba!

open

When something is closed, you open it to get inside.

Open the treasure chest to see what's inside!

out

When something is out, it is not in.

Nala, why did you go **out** of the cave?

orange

An orange is a round, orange-coloured fruit with a thick skin and a sweet taste. Oranges grow on trees.

Squeeze an **orange** to get some sweet juice!

oven

An oven is the place inside a cooker where you can bake or roast food.

Mmmm! There's a freshly baked pie in the **oven**.

owl

An owl is a bird with large, round eyes that goes "twit, twoo!"

An **owl** usually sleeps in the daytime.

83

a b c d e f g h i j k l m n **o** p q r s t u v w x y z

pyjamas

Pp

paint

When you paint something, such as a picture or a wall, you use a paintbrush to cover it with a coloured liquid.

It's fun to **paint**, isn't it, Berlioz?

paintbrush

A paintbrush is a brush that you use to paint something.

Paintbrushes come in many different sizes.

painting

A painting is a picture that someone has painted.

This is a very beautiful **painting**!

page

A page is one sheet of printed paper in a book, a magazine or a newspaper.

Turn the **page**, and let's read the rest of the story.

painter

A painter is someone who paints.

I've always wanted to be a **painter**!

pair

A pair means two of a kind.

These two are an unusual **pair**!

palette

A palette is a board on which a painter mixes paints.

How many colours of paint can you see on this **palette**?

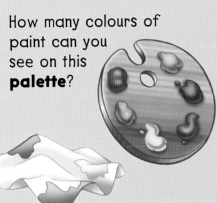

panther

A panther is a large, wild member of the cat family.

Some **panthers** are spotted, and some are black all over.

parent

A parent is the mother or the father of a child or children.

Aren't Wendy's **parents** a handsome couple?

pan

A pan is a container that people use for cooking.

Yum! Dinner is cooking in this frying **pan**!

paper

Paper is a thin material that is made from wood. We use paper for printing, writing, drawing and for wrapping parcels and other things.

The pages of this book are made of **paper**!

park

A park is the grassy place where you go to play and to enjoy being outdoors.

This **park** is a fun place to play in!

panda

A panda is a large animal with black-and-white fur. It looks like a bear.

This **panda** had never seen anyone quite like Goofy!

parade

A parade is a group of people who march together down a street to celebrate something.

There's nothing like a **parade** in Agrabah!

a b c d e f g h i j k l m n o **p** q r s t u v w x y z

parrot

A parrot is a bird with a hooked beak and bright feathers. Some parrots can talk.

What colours are the feathers of this **parrot**?

pavement

A pavement is a cement path next to a road, for people to walk along.

Do you stand on the **pavement** and watch the cars go by?

pea

A pea is a small, round, green vegetable that grows in long, thin containers called pods.

You need a spoon to eat **peas** because they roll around on the plate so much!

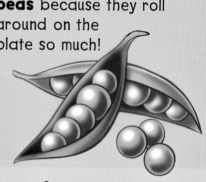

passenger

A passenger is someone who travels in a car, a bus, a train, a ship or an aeroplane.

Miss Bianca and Bernard are **passengers** on a special flight!

paw

A paw is the hand or foot of some animals.

Simba swats at a butterfly with his **paw**.

peach

A peach is a round fruit with yellow and red skin and a big stone inside. Peaches grow on trees.

A **peach** tastes good in ice cream or a pie, or on its own.

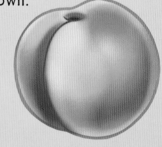

pasta

Pasta is a hard food made of flour and water. You cook pasta and eat it with a sauce.

Lady and Tramp share a romantic **pasta** dinner.

pay

When you pay for something, you give somebody money so that you can have it.

Stop right there! You have to **pay** for that apple!

pear

A pear is a bell-shaped fruit that grows on a pear tree.

When a **pear** is soft to the touch, it's ready to eat.

pen

A pen is something you use for writing or drawing. A pen is filled with coloured ink.

Belle picks up a quill **pen** to write a letter.

people

People are men, women and children.

These **people** (and their dog) make up the Darling family.

pepper

Pepper is a spice that you sprinkle on your food to make it taste better. You often use it with salt.

Achoo! If you breathe it in too deeply, **pepper** can make you sneeze.

pencil

A pencil is something you use for writing or drawing. A pencil is filled with lead.

You can rub out lines made with a **pencil**.

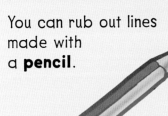

pepper

A pepper is a vegetable that can have a mild or very hot taste. Peppers can be red, green, orange or yellow.

A red **pepper** tastes a bit sweeter than a green one.

pet

A pet is an animal that lives with you and that you take care of.

penguin

A penguin is a black-and-white bird. Most penguins live in very cold places.

A **penguin** likes to slide about on ice.

Rajah, you're not just the best **pet** in the world – you're my best friend too!

a b c d e f g h i j k l m n o p q r s t u v w x y z

photograph

A photograph is a picture that you take with a camera.

Who's in that photograph?

pick up

When you pick up something, you lift it up.

The animals show Aurora a few pieces of clothing they've picked up from the forest floor.

photographer

A photographer is someone who takes pictures with a camera.

Smile! I'm the Monstropolis **photographer**!

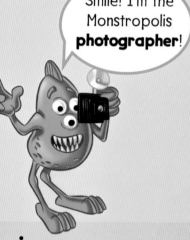

picnic

A picnic is a meal that you eat outdoors. You often sit on a rug on the ground.

Don't you just love a **picnic**?

pie

A pie is a round, baked food with a pastry crust and a filling.

Apple, rhubarb, peach and blackberry are just a few yummy **pie** fillings. Which one do you like best?

piano

A piano is a large musical instrument with 88 black-and-white keys.

You use two hands and even your feet to play the piano!

picture

You can make a picture by painting, drawing or photographing something or someone.

Can you draw a picture of a cow?

pig

A pig is an animal with a fat body, short legs and a curly tail. It goes "oink, oink!"

A pig is really a very clean and clever animal.

pillow

A pillow is a bag that is filled with something soft, such as feathers. You rest your head on a pillow while you sleep.

As soon as her head hits the **pillow**, Boo is fast asleep!

pilot

A pilot is someone who flies an aircraft.

Orville is both the **pilot** and the aeroplane!

pineapple

A pineapple is a large fruit with a thick skin and leaves. It grows in hot places.

Once you get inside the tough skin of a **pineapple**, you'll find a sweet, juicy treat!

pirate

A pirate is someone who travels on the seas to find ships to rob.

Aargh! Being a **pirate** is tough sometimes!

pizza

A pizza is a flat, round food. It is a circle of bread dough covered with tomato, cheese, meat and other foods.

Which is your favourite type of **pizza**?

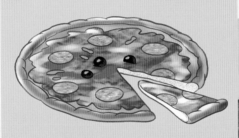

plant

A plant is any living thing that is not an animal. Plants grow in the ground.

Hello, little **plant**! I'm going to take good care of you.

plate

A plate is a round, flat dish that you serve food on.

This **plate** goes on the dinner table.

play

A play is a story that is acted out on a stage in front of an audience.

Lilo and Stich are the stars of their own **play**!

play

To play means to do things just for the fun of it.

What do you like to **play**?

a b c d e f g h i j k l m n o **p** q r s t u v w x y z

playground

A playground is an outdoor place where you go to play. It may have swings and slides.

I love going on the swings at the **playground**.

police officer

A police officer protects people from crimes.

All the **police officers** in Monstropolis are very good at their job!

police station

A police station is the place where you go to report a crime.

The **police station** is filled with police officers.

POLICE

plum

A plum is a juicy, round fruit that grows on a plum tree.

Most **plums** are green or purple.

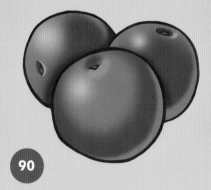

pocket

A pocket is a small cloth bag sewn into your clothing, used to carry small things.

You can keep spare change, tissues, keys and other things in a coat **pocket**.

poor

When someone is poor, it means that person has very little or no money.

We may be **poor**, Abu, but we've got each other!

popcorn

Popcorn is a snack food that is made from a type of corn. The corn puffs up when it is heated.

Popcorn tastes so good with butter and salt on it!

poster

A poster is a very large piece of paper with pictures or information on it. You hang a poster on a wall.

This is a **poster** of Daisy's favourite rock star.

pottery

Pottery is things such as plates, bowls and vases that are made out of baked clay.

Look at the pretty colours of this **pottery**!

post

The post is the letters and parcels that are delivered to you each day.

Goofy is in a hurry to deliver the **post**!

pot

A pot is a deep container that is used for cooking.

Look at all the food in that **pot**!

pour

When you pour something, you make a liquid flow in a steady stream.

Here! Allow me to **pour** you some tea – make that tea for three!

post office

A post office is the place where you go to send parcels and letters and to buy postage stamps.

Let's go to the **post office** to buy stamps.

potato

A potato is a thick vegetable that grows underground.

Whether boiled, baked, mashed or fried, a **potato** always tastes good!

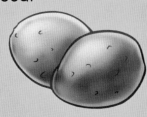

present

A present is a gift that you give to someone.

It's fun to guess what each **present** might be!

price

The price of something is the amount of money it costs to buy it.

Sulley checks the **price** of a new lunch box.

prince

A prince is the son of a sultan, a king or a queen.

Prince Phillip will do anything to save Sleeping Beauty!

princess

A princess is the daughter of a sultan, a king or a queen.

Princess Jasmine is the daughter of the Sultan of Agrabah.

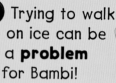
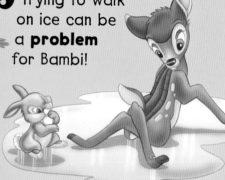

printer

A printer is a machine that is attached to a computer. It prints out on paper what you see on the screen.

Most **printers** can print in colour as well as in black and white.

problem

A problem is a difficult thing that you have to work out how to solve.

Trying to walk on ice can be a **problem** for Bambi!

pudding

A pudding is a soft, cooked, sweet food. You usually eat pudding at the end of a meal.

Do you like chocolate or vanilla **pudding** better?

pull

When you pull something, you tug it towards you.

Donald tries to **pull** the ladder down from the tree house.

pumpkin

A pumpkin is a large, round, orange fruit that grows on a vine.

Cinderella's Fairy Godmother turns a **pumpkin** into a shiny new coach!

put

To put means to place something somewhere.

Daisy wants to **put** her own umbrella up in her garden!

puppet

A puppet is a type of doll that you can move. There are glove puppets and puppets with strings.

Don't forget, **puppet**, I am the boss!

push

When you push something, you press it with your hand to move it.

Mickey **pushes** Ferdie on the swing.

puppy

A puppy is a very young dog.

This **puppy** is always hungry!

pyjamas

Pyjamas are the clothes that you sleep in. They have a top and a bottom.

Cosy **pyjamas** help you to have sweet dreams.

a b c d e f g h i j k l m n o **p** q r s t u v w x y z

93

a b c d e f g h i j k l m n o p **q** r s t u v w x y z

Qq

queen

A queen is the ruler of a country or the wife of a king.

The **Queen** of Hearts rules over Wonderland.

question

A question is something you ask when you need some information. When you ask a question, you want an answer.

So, Scuttle, here's a **question**. What is that thing?

quiet

When something is quiet, there is little or no sound.

Princess Jasmine enjoys a **quiet** moment alone.

quarrel

A quarrel is when at least two people disagree about something.

Grumpy doesn't mean to **quarrel** with the other Dwarfs. He just can't help himself!

quick

Quick is another word for fast.

Donald has to be **quick** to catch those balls!

quilt

A quilt is a cover for a bed. It has a soft filling, such as goose feathers.

A **quilt** will keep you warm on cold nights.

rope

race

A race is a competition to see who is the best at something.

Let's have a **race** back to Pride Rock!

raincoat

A raincoat is a coat that keeps the rest of your clothes dry when it rains.

Put on your **raincoat** and boots next time it rains!

rain

Rain is the drops of water that fall from clouds.

Bambi gets wet from the spring **rain**.

reach

When you reach for something, you stretch your hand out towards it.

This little lamb **reaches** out to play!

rabbit

A rabbit is an animal with soft fur, long ears and big feet. It has a short, round tail.

The name of this **rabbit** is Thumper.

rainbow

A rainbow is the wide band of colours that sometimes stretches across the sky when it has been raining.

There's always a **rainbow** in Never Land!

a b c d e f g h i j k l m n o p q **r** s t u v w x y z

read

When you read, you look at words and understand what they mean.

I can **read** a good book for hours!

referee

A referee is someone who makes sure that the rules of a game are followed.

Stitch sits high up to be the **referee** at volleyball.

remember

When you remember someone or something, you have not forgotten that person or thing.

Why can't Donald **remember** to take his money when he goes out with Daisy?

receipt

A receipt is a piece of paper that shows what you have bought and how much it cost.

Daisy has more than one **receipt** from her last shopping trip!

refrigerator

A refrigerator is a machine that keeps food cold and fresh.

Let's look in the **refrigerator** for a snack!

remote control

A remote control lets you work something, such as a television set or a toy car, from a distance.

Does your TV **remote control** sometimes get lost in the sofa cushions?

receive

When you receive something, someone gives it or delivers it to you.

Donald **receives** a lot of bills in the post!

relative

A relative is a member of your family.

The **relatives** in this family pose for a photograph.

repair

When you repair something that is broken, you mend or fix it.

Would you let Goofy **repair** your table?

reporter

A reporter is a person who collects news for a newspaper, a magazine or a radio or television station.

The Monstropolis TV **reporter** is on the air, giving the latest news.

restaurant

A restaurant is a place where people go to eat. You pay for your meals in a restaurant.

I like everything to be perfect before I open my **restaurant**.

rhinoceros

A rhinoceros is a large animal with thick skin and one or two horns on its nose.

The **rhinoceros** is found in Africa and Asia.

rich

Someone who is rich has a lot of money.

I'm **rich, rich, rich**! And it's all mine!

right

Right is the opposite direction to left.

Nala, I am on your **right** side.

ribbon

A ribbon is a long, thin strip of material, paper or plastic. You use a ribbon to tie something together.

A present looks prettier with a **ribbon** on it!

ride

When you ride in or on something, you move along with it.

Stitch **rides** a bike in a really crazy way!

right

Right is also the opposite of wrong. If you do something the right way, you do it correctly.

That's the **right** answer. Very good work!

rice

Rice is a grain that is grown as food in warm, wet places.

Can you use chopsticks to eat **rice**?

river

A river is a large stream of moving water that flows from a high place, such as a mountain, to a lower place, such as the sea.

A **river** runs quietly next to Mickey's camp site.

a b c d e f g h i j k l m n o p q **r** s t u v w x y z

rock

A rock is the hard material that makes up mountains, hills and the ground.

Rafiki presents Baby Simba for the first time at Pride **Rock**!

ruler

A ruler is a long, flat piece of wood, metal or plastic. You use it to measure the length of something.

A **ruler** can help you to draw a straight line.

roll

When something rolls, it moves by turning over and over.

Sir Hiss **rolls** down the hill in his own special way!

rope

A rope is a strong, thick string.

A **rope** can come in handy on a camping trip.

run

When you run, you use your legs to move quickly.

I'll **run** all the way home with you, Simba!

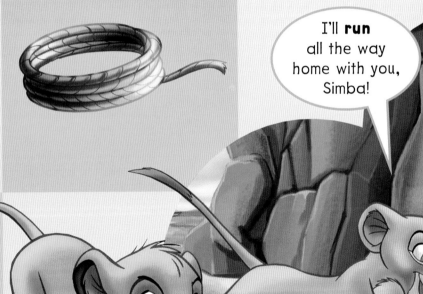

roof

A roof is the covering on top of a building or a vehicle such as a car or a train.

The **roof** on Mickey's house is bright red!

a
b
c
d
e
f
g
h
i
j
k
l
m
n
o
p
q
r
s
t
u
v
w
x
y
z

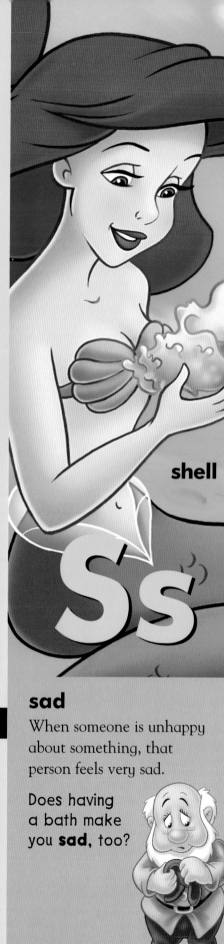

shell

Ss

sail

When you sail, you travel in a boat that has sails.

Ariel watches Eric's ship **sail**.

salad

A salad is a mixture of vegetables such as lettuce and tomatoes. You usually eat them cold and uncooked.

Here's a crisp, fresh **salad**.

same

When something is the same as something else, it means that the things are alike.

Ha, ha! We're wearing the **same** dress!

sad

When someone is unhappy about something, that person feels very sad.

Does having a bath make you **sad**, too?

salt

Salt is a white powder or white grains that come out of the ground or the sea. You add salt to food to make it taste better.

Every kitchen has a **salt** pot.

sand

Sand is made of tiny pieces of rock. You find sand on beaches and in hot desert.

Uh-oh! So much **sand** and no Aladdin – and no banana!

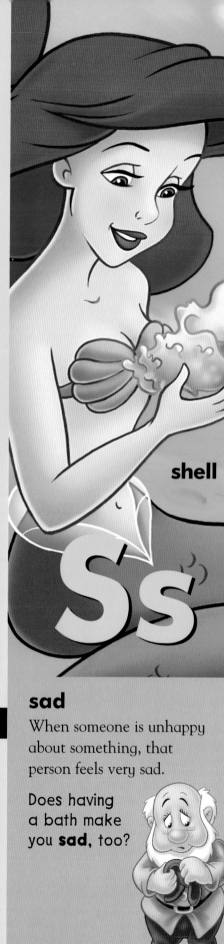

a b c d e f g h i j k l m n o p q r **s** t u v w x y z

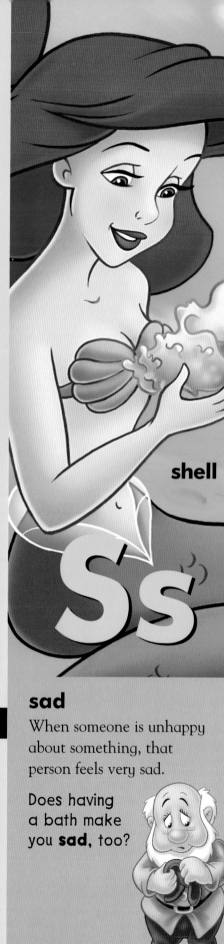

100

sandal

A sandal is a shoe with lots of open spaces to keep your feet cool in warm weather.

Your toes can wiggle "hello" to the sun when you wear **sandals**.

sandwich

A sandwich is two pieces of bread with some kind of filling.

What kind of **sandwich** do you like to eat?

sausage

A sausage is a mixture of meat and spices that are rolled up together.

Sausages taste good whether they're boiled or fried.

sandcastle

A sandcastle is a building that you make out of sand.

Oh, no! Stitch is stamping on a **sandcastle!**

saucer

A saucer is a small dish that is made to hold a cup.

This **saucer** is a perfect fit for me!

save

When you save something, you keep it because you want to have it later.

Huey, Dewey and Louie **save** money for Uncle Donald's birthday present.

sandpit

A sandpit is a big outdoor area that is filled with sand. It's fun to play in a sandpit.

You can dig for hours in a **sandpit!**

saw

A saw is a long tool with many sharp teeth. A saw is used to cut pieces of wood.

A **saw** moves backwards and forwards across the wood that it's cutting.

a b c d e f g h i j k l m n o p q r **s** t u v w x y z

saxophone

A saxophone is a musical instrument that is shaped like the letter S.

The Scat Cat Band always has a **saxophone** player!

scarf

A scarf is a long piece of material, usually wool, that you wrap around your neck to keep warm.

The **scarf** is longer than the mouse!

scissors

A pair of scissors is a tool that you use to cut things.

You can use safety **scissors** to cut fun shapes out of paper.

say

When you say something, you speak words.

We want to **say** goodbye! Thanks for coming!

scary

When something is scary, a person is afraid of it.

Everyone thinks Ursula the sea witch is **scary**!

scratch

When you scratch something, you rub it with something sharp, such as your fingernails.

Let me **scratch** that itch for you!

scared

If you are scared, it means you are afraid of something.

Sulley was **scared** when Boo pulled his tail.

school

A school is a place where you go to learn many exciting new things.

Today's lesson at **school** is about shapes!

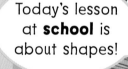

scream

When you scream, you make a very loud sound with your voice, without using words.

Some people **scream** when they watch scary films.

sea

A sea is a large area of salty water. Seas cover about three-quarters of the world.

Lilo and Stitch are almost ready to surf in the **sea**!

screen

The screen of your computer is the glass part that shows the words and pictures.

Whose face is on the **screen**?

seafood

Seafood includes all the animals that live in the sea and that people eat.

Shrimps, fish and lobsters are **seafood**.

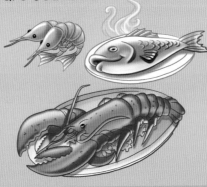

seal

A seal is an animal that lives in and around the sea. It uses its flippers to move around.

This **seal** has a special talent!

screwdriver

A screwdriver is a tool that pushes screws into wood.

Hold the **screwdriver** by the handle and turn it slowly.

seagull

A seagull is a large, white bird that lives near the sea and feeds on fish.

Now hear this! Scuttle the **seagull** has something to say!

a b c d e f g h i j k l m n o p q r **s** t u v w x y z

seasons

A season is one of the four different parts of the year: spring, summer, autumn and winter.

Which **season** do you like the best?

Spring

The rain in **spring** tastes good!

Summer

I just love the flowers that bloom in **summer**!

Autumn

It's very windy in **autumn**!

Winter

There's lots of slippery ice in **winter**!

second

There are 60 seconds in one minute.

Lilo counts the number of **seconds** that she can hold her breath.

secret

A secret is something that you don't want everyone to know.

Daisy whispers a **secret** in Donald's ear.

secretary

A secretary is someone who types letters and keeps records for someone else.

A **secretary** works in an office.

see

When you look at something with your eyes, you can see it.

I never thought I'd **see** this!

sew

When you sew, you use a needle and thread to join pieces of material together.

Let's **sew** this bow onto Cinderella's dress!

shake

When you shake something, you move it up and down or from side to side very quickly.

Sebastian will **shake** anything to see if it makes music!

sell

When you sell something, you let someone else have it for money.

Roger will never **sell** his puppies to Cruella De Vil!

shadow

When you stand in the sun, the dark shape that your body makes on the ground is called your shadow.

Little John has a big **shadow**.

shampoo

Shampoo is the liquid soap you use to wash your hair.

Shampoo has a clean, fresh smell.

send

When you send something, you make it go from one place to another.

Let's **send** this far away!

a b c d e f g h i j k l m n o p q r **s** t u v w x y z

shape

The shape of something is what the outside of it looks like.

Do you have a favourite **shape**?

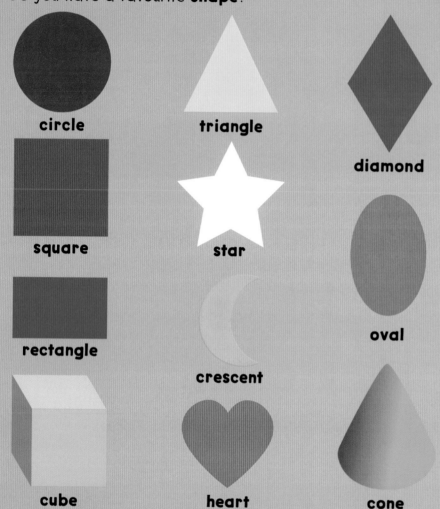

circle

triangle

diamond

square

star

rectangle

oval

crescent

cube

heart

cone

sharp

Something that is sharp has a pointed tip or an edge that can cut.

Captain Hook has a very **sharp** sword!

shave

When a man shaves, he uses a razor to trim the hair on his face.

Captain Hook lets Smee **shave** his face.

share

When you share something, you give part of it to someone else.

Oliver and Tito **share** one side of the see-saw.

shark

A shark is a large fish with a big mouth and rows of sharp teeth.

Look at the big teeth on this **shark**!

sheep

A sheep is an animal with four legs and curly fur called wool. Sheep go "baa, baa!"

Every spring, it's time to shear the **sheep** for their wool.

sheet

A sheet is a thin, flat piece of material that covers your bed.

This bed has soft, white **sheets** and a blanket.

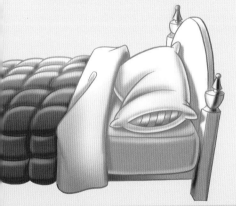

shelf

A shelf is a place on a wall or in a cupboard where you can put things.

What would you put on the **shelf**?

shell

A shell is a hard covering that protects things such as eggs and nuts, and animals such as turtles and clams.

Ariel finds many pretty **shells** on the beach.

shine

If something shines, it gives off light.

The sun **shines** brightly on Daisy!

ship

A ship is a large boat.

This **ship** is going on a long journey.

shirt

A shirt is a piece of clothing that covers you from your neck down to your waist.

This **shirt** has beautiful buttons.

shoe

You wear a shoe on your foot over your sock.

Don't you just love my pink **shoes**?

short

Short means not long.

Alice is so **short** that she fits under the table.

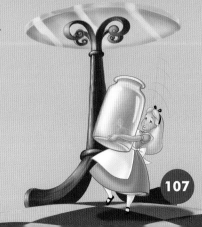

a b c d e f g h i j k l m n o p q r **s** t u v w x y z

shorts

Shorts are trousers that only come down to your knees.

Those are some fancy **shorts**!

show

When you show people something, you point it out to them.

Come on, Sulley. Just **show** me who you're hiding in there!

shout

When someone shouts, that person calls out or yells in a very loud voice.

Timothy **shouts** to Dumbo!

shower

When you have a shower, you wash yourself while you stand under streams of water.

Goofy always sings when he has a **shower**.

shy

A shy person is someone who is quiet in front of other people.

Snow White doesn't mind that Bashful is **shy**.

shovel

A shovel is a type of spade with a long handle and a big scoop. You use a shovel to lift snow and sand.

It's handy to have a **shovel** when you clear away the snow.

shut

When you shut something, you close something that was open.

Sir Hiss thinks King John has **shut** the chest too quickly!

sign

A sign is a word, a mark or a picture that give you information about something.

This **sign** shows the monster where the bus stop is.

singer

A singer is a person who sings.

For a real **singer**, just call a Scat Cat!

sit

When you sit down, you are no longer standing up.

Belle **sits** down to read her favourite book.

silver

Silver is an expensive grey metal that is used to make jewellery and other things.

Some knives, forks and spoons are made of **silver**.

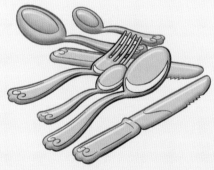

sink

A sink is a container in your kitchen that you can fill with water. You do the washing-up in a sink.

This **sink** is rather full!

skateboard

A skateboard is a long, flat piece of wood on wheels. You move on it by pushing one foot along the ground.

When you learn to ride a **skateboard**, be sure to wear safety gear!

sing

When you sing, you make music with your voice.

Goofy **sings** his own special song!

sister

Your sister is the female child of your parents.

I'm glad you're my **sister**, Nani!

a b c d e f g h i j k l m n o p q r **s** t u v w x y z

109

ski

To ski means to come down a snowy hill on skis.

This is the first time the Beast has tried to **ski**.

ski

A ski is a long, flat piece of wood, metal or plastic that you use to ski over snow. You fasten it to a special boot.

Donald is not so good on **skis**!

skip

When you skip, you move by jumping and hopping along, one foot at a time.

Pinocchio **skips** off to school.

skirt

A skirt is a piece of clothing that girls and women wear. It begins at the waist and hangs around the legs.

This is a lovely **skirt** for the spring.

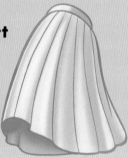

sky

The sky is what you see when you are outside and look up.

The night **sky** is full of stars.

skyscraper

A skyscraper is a very tall building with many floors.

There are a lot of **skyscrapers** in a city.

sledge

A sledge is a flat board with blades under it. You sit on a sledge to move down snowy hills.

You can pull parcels home on your **sledge**.

sleep

When you sleep, you relax with your eyes closed. You stop moving and thinking, and you begin to dream.

The Beast can **sleep** anywhere!

sleeping bag

A sleeping bag is a cosy, warm bag made of soft material. You zip yourself into it when you sleep outdoors.

It's time to climb into your **sleeping bag**!

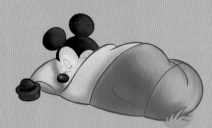

slide

A slide is an object in a playground. It has a ladder that you climb up, and a long, shiny part that you slide down.

Whee! It's fun to go down a **slide**!

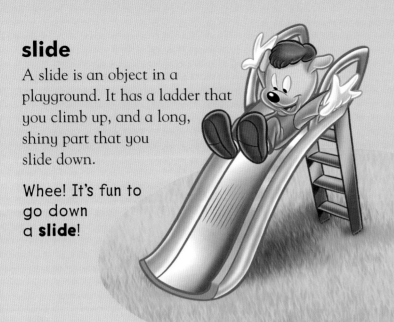

smell

When you smell something, you use your nose to find out about it.

Minnie can't **smell** anything because she has a cold.

slipper

A slipper is a soft shoe that you wear at home, usually when you're in your pyjamas.

These **slippers** will keep your feet warm and snug.

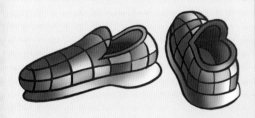

small

If something is small, it doesn't take up much space.

Abu doesn't like being so **small**.

smile

When you smile, your mouth turns up at the corners. You smile when you're happy.

Smile for the camera!

slow

Slow is the opposite of fast.

Be glad that I'm **slow**, monkey!

smart

Someone who looks smart is very clean and tidy.

The doorman looks so **smart** in his fine uniform.

a b c d e f g h i j k l m n o p q r **s** t u v w x y z

smoke

Smoke is the cloud that rises from something that is burning.

Smoke is rising from that campfire.

snake

A snake is a long, thin animal with no legs. Snakes slither along the ground.

There are **snakes** all over the world, except in Ireland.

snowball

A snowball is a hard, round lump of snow.

I'm so cross! Take that! A **snowball**!

snack

A snack is something that you eat between meals.

Timon enjoys a crunchy **snack**!

sneeze

When you sneeze, you make a noise as lots of air rushes out of your nose and mouth.

Achoo! When Lumiere **sneezes** he makes a lot of noise.

snail

A snail is a small animal with a round shell on its back. Snails move along very slowly.

Goofy is very close to that **snail**!

snow

Snow is the soft, white flakes of ice that sometimes fall from the clouds when it is very cold.

Belle loves the falling **snow**.

snowboard

A snowboard is a flat piece of fibreglass or plastic. You stand or sit on it to slide down a snowy hill.

Donald can balance on a **snowboard** really well!

soccer

Soccer is another name for football. It is a game played by two teams, which try to kick the ball into each other's goal.

Mickey and Goofy are playing **soccer**.

snowflake

A snowflake is a single piece of snow. No two snowflakes are exactly the same.

Pluto leaps to catch a **snowflake**.

soap

Soap is what you use when you wash yourself to become clean.

That's a big bar of **soap**!

sock

A sock is a piece of clothing that you wear on your foot, under your shoe. Socks come in pairs.

These **socks** match, so they can't belong to Goofy!

snowman

A snowman is made out of big balls of snow.

Lumiere is melting the **snowman**!

soapsud

A soapsud is one of the bubbles that appear when you mix soap and water together.

Lilo's friend, Stitch, is covered in **soapsuds**!

a b c d e f g h i j k l m n o p q r **s** t u v w x y z

sofa

A sofa is a long, soft piece of furniture that one or more people can sit on.

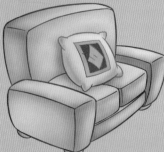

A **sofa** is a comfy place to sit and watch TV.

soft

When something is soft, it means it is not hard.

Grumpy wishes he had a **soft** pillow too.

soggy

When something is soggy, it is very wet.

Donald is looking a bit **soggy**!

someone

Someone means somebody.

Someone is sleeping on the cushion.

something

When you talk about something you do not say exactly what you mean.

Pluto sees **something** he wants!

son

A son is the male child of his parents.

Lady and Tramp have a **son** who looks like his father.

song

A song is the music that you make with your voice.

These are the notes to a beautiful **song**.

soon

If something is going to happen soon, it means it will happen a short time from now.

Mickey had better get here **soon**!

spaceship

A spaceship is a machine that travels into space from the Earth. It is powered by a rocket motor.

Lilo likes the **spaceship** ride more than Stitch does!

soup

Soup is a hot, liquid food that is made from water or milk and other things, such as meat and vegetables.

Hot **soup** warms you up on a cold winter's day.

spider

A spider is a small animal with eight legs, which spins webs.

Look at the **spider** hanging from its web!

spoon

A spoon has a little scoop at the end of a handle. You use it to eat soft or wet foods.

You eat soup with a **spoon**.

south

South is the direction that is the opposite of north.

On a map, the **south** is towards the bottom.

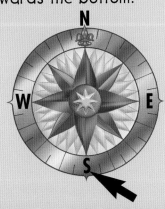

spinach

Spinach is a dark green, leafy vegetable.

Spinach is good for you.

spot

A spot is a small mark on something.

Look at all the **spots** on this puppy!

squirrel

A squirrel is a small, furry animal with a bushy tail. Squirrels live in trees and eat nuts.

The **squirrels** are friends with Aurora.

star

A star is a twinkling light that you can see in the night sky. Stars are made up of gases.

Simba looks up at the **stars** when he thinks about his father, Mufasa.

stable

A stable is a place where a horse is kept.

This horse has left its **stable** to gallop around the field.

stamp

A stamp is a small piece of paper that you stick onto a letter or parcel when you post it.

Make sure you put a **stamp** on your letter!

stage

A stage is the raised area in a theatre where actors, musicians and dancers perform in front of an audience.

This **stage** even has palm trees!

stand

To stand means to be up on your feet.

Belle **stands** in her new dress and shoes.

start

When you start something, you begin to do it.

We'll **start** dinner once you've washed your hands!

stay

To stay somewhere means to remain there.

Let's **stay** at home and have fun!

stop

When you stop doing something, you don't do it anymore.

Stop the car, Goofy! It's the elephant's turn to cross the road!

steak

A steak is a slice of cooked beef.

Potatoes and peas go well with **steak**.

stork

A stork is a large bird with a big beak and very long legs.

This **stork** is standing on one leg only!

storm

A storm is a type of bad weather, with rain or snow and usually a lot of wind.

Come, children. Let's get out of this **storm**.

stepmother

A stepmother is a woman who marries your father but she is not your mother.

Cinderella's wicked **stepmother** wants the Prince to marry one of her daughters.

storybook

A storybook is a children's book with words and pictures.

This **storybook** has lots of stories about magical people and places.

117

a b c d e f g h i j k l m n o p q r **s** t u v w x y z

strange

Something that is strange is unusual and different.

Even the Queen of Hearts thinks the Cheshire Cat is **strange**!

strawberry

A strawberry is a small, red fruit with lots of seeds. A strawberry plant grows close to the ground.

Fresh **strawberries** are so sweet and juicy!

stretch

When you stretch, you spread your arms, legs and body out to full length.

Berlioz's nap is over when Toulouse decides to **stretch**.

stream

A stream is a small river.

The water in this **stream** is clear blue!

string

String is a very thin type of rope.

String often comes in a long roll.

straw

A straw is a long, narrow paper or plastic tube that you use to drink something.

Suck in your cheeks when you drink through a **straw**!

street

A street is a road, usually with buildings on each side, that cars drive along.

The cats chase Donald up the middle of the **street**!

stripe

A stripe is a line of colour.

The Cheshire Cat's fur is full of colourful **stripes**!

student

A student is someone who is learning something.

Mortie and Ferdie are **students** in Goofy's class.

suitcase

A suitcase is a container with a handle. You pack your clothes in a suitcase when you travel.

This **suitcase** is jammed full of clothes!

strong

If someone is strong, that person has a lot of power.

I knew you were **strong** enough to hold all these books.

sugar

Sugar is a white or brown food that makes drinks and food taste sweeter.

Sugar comes in either grains or cubes.

sun

The sun is a star that sends light and heat to Earth.

The **sun** shines during the daytime.

suit

A suit is a matching set of clothes, such as trousers or a skirt paired with a jacket.

Look at this smart, new **suit**!

sunbathe

To sunbathe means to lie out in the sun.

Nani **sunbathes** during her day off .

a b c d e f g h i j k l m n o p q r **s** t u v w x y z

sunglasses

Sunglasses are dark glasses that you wear to protect your eyes from too much sunshine.

Sunglasses are good to have at the beach.

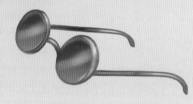

sunrise

Sunrise is the time when the sun comes up in the morning.

At **sunrise**, Rafiki lifts baby Simba for all the animals to see.

sunset

Sunset is the time when the sun goes down.

Simba and Nala enjoy the **sunset** together.

sunshine

Sunshine is the light and heat that we get from the sun.

The **sunshine** is too strong, even for a Genie, today!

suntan lotion

Suntan lotion is a liquid that you put on your skin to protect it from being burned by too much sunshine.

Before you sit in the sun, rub in lots of **suntan lotion**!

surf

To surf means to ride on a surfboard.

That guy really knows how to **surf**!

surfboard

A surfboard is a plastic board that you stand on while you ride along the waves.

You need to have good balance on a **surfboard**.

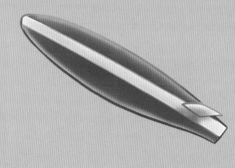

surprised

If you are surprised by something, it means that you weren't expecting it.

Cinderella is so **surprised**!

swim

When you swim, you use your hands and feet to move through the water.

I love to **swim**!

sweater

A sweater is a knitted piece of clothing that you wear to keep warm.

This **sweater** is yellow and purple.

swimsuit

A swimsuit is a piece of clothing that you wear when you go in the water.

Fetch your **swimsuit** and let's go swimming!

sword

A sword is a weapon with a handle that is joined to a long piece of metal with sharp edges.

I'll use this **sword** to slay Maleficent!

sweet

Something tastes sweet if it has sugar or honey in it.

Mickey gives a **sweet** heart to his sweetheart.

swing

A swing is a seat that swings from ropes or chains. You sit on it and move your legs up and down.

Mortie and Ferdie go on the **swings** in the park.

a b c d e f g h i j k l m n o p q r **s** t u v w x y z

toothbrush

Tt

tablecloth

A tablecloth is a piece of material that covers a table.

Clarabelle doesn't want Horace to spill on the **tablecloth** when he makes his sandwich.

tail

A tail is something that some animals grow at the lower end of their back.

This monkey uses his **tail** like an extra hand!

talk

When you talk, you say words out loud.

Shh! Don't **talk**! Let me explain.

table

A table is a piece of furniture with a flat top, and legs to hold it up.

The **table** is set for a romantic dinner.

take

To take something means to get it by reaching for it.

Baloo and Mowgli will **take** some bananas from the tree.

tall

When someone is tall, there is a long distance between the head and the feet of that person.

How did Dopey get to be so **tall**?

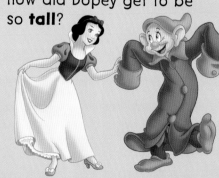

tambourine

A tambourine is a round musical instrument that you hit. It has metal discs around the edges that jingle when you shake it.

Bang on the **tambourine** and then shake, shake, shake it!

taxi

A taxi is a car driven by a taxi driver. You pay the driver to take you to places.

Some **taxis** have meters in them that tell you the fare.

teapot

A teapot is a container with a handle and a spout. You make and serve tea in a teapot.

I don't really mind being a **teapot,** love!

taste

Taste is one of the five senses. It lets you know what something you eat is made of.

A small **taste** is packed with hot spices!

tea

Tea is a hot liquid that people drink. It is made with water and the dried leaves of certain plants.

Some people like lemon in their **tea**.

tear

When something tears, it is pulled apart.

The crocodile waits for Captain Hook's coat to **tear**.

taste

When you taste something, you put a little bit of it in your mouth to see if you like it.

Pumbaa loves to **taste** his food!

teacher

A teacher is someone who helps you to learn new things.

Your **teacher** knows a lot of things!

a b c d e f g h i j k l m n o p q r s **t** u v w x y z

123

teddy bear

A teddy bear is a stuffed animal in the shape of a bear.

I sleep with my **teddy bear** every night.

tell

When you tell someone something, you are sharing something you know.

Tell me what to do, Grandmother Willow!

tennis

Tennis is a game where players use a tennis racket to hit a tennis ball backwards and forwards over a net.

Minnie enjoys a good game of **tennis**.

telephone

A telephone is a machine that lets you talk to someone who is not in the same place as you.

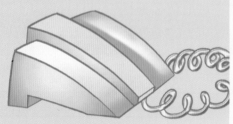

Brring! Brring! The **telephone** is ringing.

temper

Your temper is the mood that you're in. Someone with a bad temper gets angry easily.

Donald has a really bad **temper**.

tent

A tent is an outdoor shelter that is made of strong material and poles.

It's fun to sleep in a **tent** when you're camping.

television

A television shows pictures on a screen while it plays sounds.

The puppies are ready in front of the **television** to watch their favourite programme!

test

When you take a test, you answer questions to show how well you know something.

Donald thinks the **test** is hard!

thermometer

A thermometer is something that measures the temperature of a person or a place.

Can you read the **thermometer**?

think

When you think, you use your mind.

Aladdin **thinks** about Jasmine too much, according to Abu.

through

Through means from one end to the other.

Simba and Nala run **through** the valley.

thick

When something is thick, it is not thin.

One of you has a very **thick** tail!

thirsty

If you are thirsty, it means you need something to drink.

Timothy and Dumbo are very **thirsty**.

throw

When you throw something, you use your hands to make it fly through the air.

Roger **throws** a stick for his pal Pongo.

thin

If a person doesn't weigh much, he or she is thin.

Aladdin is a **thin**, young man.

a b c d e f g h i j k l m n o p q r s **t** u v w x y z

thunder

Thunder is the loud noise that comes from the sky soon after you see lightning.

The **thunder** scares Mike.

tidy

When something is tidy, it means that it is neat.

Lilo's room isn't very **tidy**!

tie

To tie something means to hold it together.

You **tie** a tie around your neck!

time

Time is how long it takes for something to happen. Time is also the hours and minutes on a clock that show where you are in your day.

Oh, no! The **time** is midnight!

ticket

A ticket is a piece of paper that you buy when you go on a train or a bus, or go into places such as cinemas.

Buy your **ticket**, and let's go in!

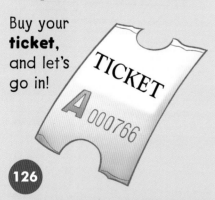
TICKET
A 000766

tiger

A tiger is the largest wild cat. It has orange or white fur with dark stripes.

Tigers, like all cats, spend a lot of time sleeping.

tin

Tin is a metal that is used to make cans.

This **tin** can is filled with tomatoes.

tired

You are tired if you are sleepy or need to rest.

When Timon is **tired,** he has a good place to rest!

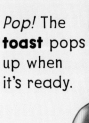

toaster

A toaster is an electric machine that heats bread to turn it into toast.

This **toaster** can toast two slices of bread at a time.

toilet

A toilet is a bowl with water that you sit on to get rid of your body's waste. You then flush the toilet.

The **toilet** is in the bathroom.

tissue

A tissue is a soft piece of paper that you use to wipe something with.

You wipe your nose with a **tissue** when you have a cold.

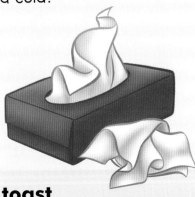

today

Today means this day.

Today is Mickey's birthday!

tomato

A tomato is a bright-red fruit that grows on a vine and has seeds inside it.

A sliced **tomato** is good in sandwiches and salads.

toast

Toast is bread that has been heated in a toaster until it is brown and crunchy.

Pop! The **toast** pops up when it's ready.

together

Together means with someone or something.

Boo, Sulley and Mike always have lots of fun **together**.

a b c d e f g h i j k l m n o p q r s **t** u v w x y z

Alphabet sidebar
a
b
c
d
e
f
g
h
i
j
k
l
m
n
o
p
q
r
s
t
u
v
w
x
y
z

tomorrow

Tomorrow is the day after today.

Goodbye! I'll see you **tomorrow**!

toothbrush

You brush your teeth with a toothbrush.

You move your **toothbrush** up and down across your teeth when you clean them.

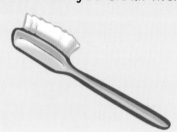

tortoise

A tortoise is a big turtle that lives on land and moves very slowly.

The **tortoise**, like all turtles, has a hard shell on its back.

tonight

Tonight is this evening. It is the time that begins after the afternoon.

Tonight is for lovers!

toothpaste

You put toothpaste on your toothbrush to help clean and polish your teeth.

Be sure to squeeze the **toothpaste** tube gently!

touch

When you touch something, you use your hand to feel it.

No, Sleeping Beauty! Don't **touch** the spindle!

towel

A towel is a thick piece of soft material that you use to dry things.

This **towel** has pictures of shells on it.

tower

A tower is a very tall, thin building.

This castle has a lot of **towers**.

toy

A toy is something that you play with, such as a doll or a ball.

The puppies share a **toy**.

toy box

You keep your favourite toys in a toy box.

This **toy box** is full.

toy shop

A toy shop is a place that sells toys.

Look at all the things in the **toy shop**!

tractor

A tractor is a big machine that is used to pull farm machines or heavy loads.

This **tractor** helps a farmer to do his jobs.

traffic

Traffic means all the cars, lorries, buses and other machines that drive on the road at one time.

Oliver and Dodger find a way to miss the **traffic**!

traffic light

A traffic light lets people and traffic know when it's their turn to move and when to stop and wait.

Yep, the **traffic light** tells me I can cross now!

a b c d e f g h i j k l m n o p q r s **t** u v w x y z

train

A train is a row of carriages that are joined to each other and pulled by an engine. It moves along a railway track.

This is quite an old-fashioned **train**!

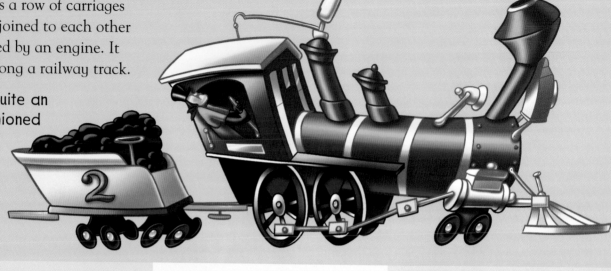

tray

A tray is a flat piece of a hard material, such as metal or plastic, on which you carry things.

You can carry a lot of things on this **tray**!

tree

A tree is a large and very tall plant with deep roots, a trunk and branches.

That old buzzard won't find me in this **tree**!

REWARD

Robin Hood

trip

When you go on a trip you travel somewhere, often for a holiday.

Flik is going on a **trip** to the mountains.

treasure

Treasure is a collection of valuable things.

There's quite a lot of **treasure** in that chest!

trombone

A trombone is a musical instrument that is made of brass. It has a part that you slide up and down to make different sounds.

It helps to have long arms to play the **trombone**!

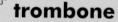
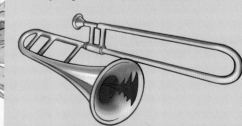

trophy

A trophy is an award that you get for doing well in a sport or some other event.

This **trophy** is for the first-place winner!

trumpet

A trumpet is a musical instrument that is made of brass. It has three keys that you press down to make different sounds.

Thomas O'Malley has heard enough of the **trumpet**!

truth

When you tell the truth, you are saying how things really are.

Tell me the **truth**, son. What happened?

turn

When you turn something, you move it in a different direction or in a circle.

Flik **turns** his flying machine towards the enemy grasshoppers.

trunk

The trunk of an elephant is its long nose.

An elephant lifts its **trunk** when it is happy.

twins

Twins are two people who were born at the same time to the same mother and father. Some twins look exactly alike.

Can you tell that we're **twins**?

131

a b c d e f g h i j k l m n o p q r s **t** u v w x y z

umbrella

a b c d e f g h i j k l m n o p q r s t **u** v w x y z

umbrella

An umbrella is a round piece of material on a handle that you open to stop rain from falling on you.

My **umbrella** is blue like a clear sky.

understand

If you understand something, you know what it means.

I don't **understand** these signs!

uncle

Your uncle is the brother of your father or mother.

Donald is the **uncle** of three noisy nephews!

uniform

A uniform is a special type of clothing that shows you what job someone does, such as a police officer or a firefighter.

This is a firefighter's **uniform**.

ugly

Something that is ugly is unpleasant to look at.

The Evil Witch is *sooo* **ugly**!

under

When something is under something else, it is below it.

Simba is **under** Nala.

up

When something goes up, it goes from a lower to a higher place.

Mickey and Goofy jump **up** from the sofa to cheer!

violin

Vv

vet

A vet is a doctor who looks after animals when they are ill.

It can be rewarding but tough to be a **vet**!

video game

A video game is a game that you play on a special video game player.

Video games are fun for the whole family!

VCR

A VCR, or video recorder, is a machine that you use to record television programmes. You can watch them whenever you want.

Let's put a tape in the **VCR** and watch it together!

visit

When you visit someone, you go somewhere to see that person.

Uncle Scrooge has come to **visit** Donald.

voice

Your voice is the sound you make when you talk or sing.

The birds love Cinderella's **voice**.

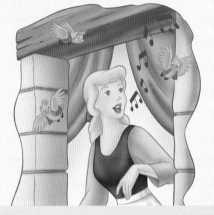

violin

A violin is a musical instrument with four strings that you play with a bow.

Every orchestra has lots of **violins**.

volleyball

Volleyball is a game played by two teams on a court. Players hit a ball over a net with their hands.

Slam! The ball goes over the **volleyball** net!

a b c d e f g h i j k l m n o p q r s t u v w x y z

a b c d e f g h i j k l m n o p q r s t u v w x y z

woman

Ww

waiter

A waiter takes your order and brings your meal to you in a restaurant.

Would you like Goofy to be your **waiter**?

wake up

When you wake up, you are no longer asleep.

It's time to **wake up**, Belle!

wallet

A wallet is a flat, folded container in which you keep money, photographs, bank cards and other things.

Tuck your home address into your **wallet**.

walk

When you walk, you move by placing one foot in front of the other.

I'd love to **walk** with you!

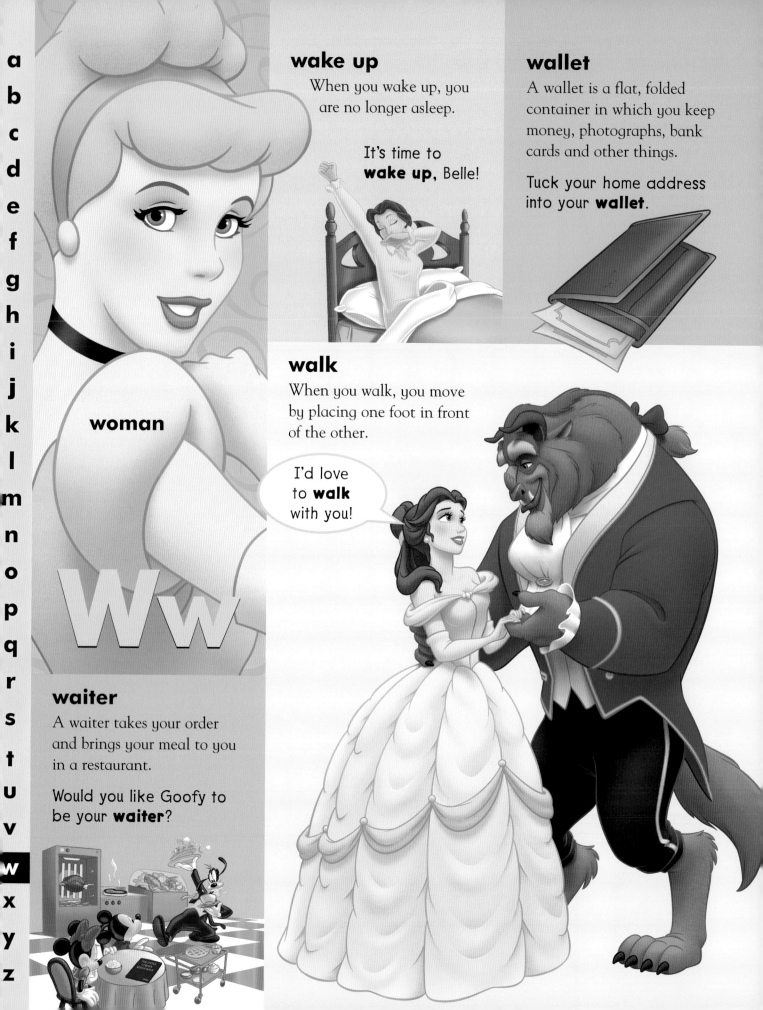

want

If you want something, you would like to have it. If you want to do something, you would like to do it.

I **want** that lamp, Abu!

washing machine

A washing machine uses water, soap powder and electricity to wash clothes.

A **washing machine** is used to wash clothes, not lorries, silly!

water

When you water a plant or a lawn, you pour water on it to help it grow.

Cinderella **waters** her pretty little plants.

wardrobe

A wardrobe is a big cupboard that holds your clothes.

Daisy has a very full **wardrobe**.

watch

A watch is a small clock that you wear around your wrist.

Look at your **watch** to see what time it is now.

waterfall

A waterfall is a wide stream of water that falls from a high to a low place.

Whoosh! You can hear the water rushing down the **waterfall**.

wash

When you wash something, you use water, and often soap, to clean it.

The animals watch Snow White **wash** her clothes.

water

Water is the clear liquid that comes from rain and melting snow, or from seas, rivers and lakes.

Ariel just loves the **water**!

watermelon

A watermelon is a large, juicy fruit with a green skin and lots of seeds inside it.

Yum! **Watermelon** is a sweet summer snack.

wear

To wear something means to be dressed in some sort of clothing.

*I always **wear** fur!*

weigh

You weigh things to find out how heavy or light they are.

Daisy cannot believe she **weighs** that much!

wave

When you wave at someone, you move your hand to say hello or goodbye.

Lilo **waves** when she's happy to see someone.

wedding

A wedding is when two people get married.

Cinderella and her Prince had the most beautiful **wedding**!

weak

Weak means not strong.

Donald is too **weak** to carry all that money.

weekend

Saturday and Sunday are the days of the weekend.

Snow White bakes a special pie for the **weekend**.

west

West is the direction that is the opposite of east. On a map, west is on the left side.

The sun sets in the **west**.

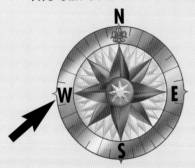

whisper

When you whisper, you talk in a very quiet voice, so that only the person you are talking to can hear you.

Can you hear Belle **whisper** to the Beast?

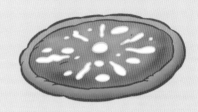

whole

If something is whole, it means it is all there and that none of it is missing.

Do you think you could eat a **whole** pizza?

wet

When something is wet, it means it has water in it or on it.

Ha! Rajah, you look so funny when you're all **wet**!

whistle

A whistle is a small instrument that makes a loud sound. You put it in your mouth and blow on it.

Fweet! Fweet! That **whistle** is loud!

wide

If something is wide, it takes up a lot of space from one side to the other.

Sorry, Pumbaa, but it's not **wide** enough!

whale

A whale is the largest animal that lives in the sea.

A **whale** lives in the sea but comes up to the surface to breathe air.

wife

A wife is a woman who is married.

Fa Li is the **wife** of Fa Zhou.

a b c d e f g h i j k l m n o p q r s t u v **w** x y z

win

When you win a contest or a game, it means that you finish in first place.

It looks as if they both **win** something!

woman

A girl becomes a woman.

Aurora is a beautiful young **woman**.

wind

Wind is the air that you can feel when it is moving fast.

Pocahontas loves the feel of the **wind** going through her hair.

wing

A wing is the part of a bird or an aeroplane that helps it to fly.

A bird flaps its **wings** – then up it goes!

wolf

A wolf is a wild animal that looks like a large dog and howls in the night.

This **wolf** is looking for the Three Little Pigs.

wood

Wood is something that you use to make doors, windows, chairs and other things. It comes from the trunk and branches of a tree.

This table is made from planks of **wood**.

work

Work is the type of job that you do.

We love our **work**!

writer

A writer is a person whose job it is to make up stories or give you information by using words.

Belle wants to be a **writer** of great books.

worst

Worst is the opposite of best.

Pumbaa thinks rain is the **worst** kind of weather.

wrong

If something is wrong, it is not correct.

Without a doubt, this is the **wrong** foot.

write

When you write, you put words down on paper.

Mulan **writes** a letter to her grandmother.

a
b
c
d
e
f
g
h
i
j
k
l
m
n
o
p
q
r
s
t
u
v
w
x
y
z

X-ray

yoghurt

zip

Xx   Yy   Zz

X-ray

An X-ray is a photograph of the inside of someone's body.

This **X-ray** shows how bones fit together.

xylophone

A xylophone is a musical instrument made of narrow strips of metal or plastic that you hit to make different sounds.

Here's an under-the-sea **xylophone**!

yawn

You yawn when you are sleepy by opening your mouth wide and slowly breathing in and out.

Sometimes you might **yawn** when you're bored.

year

A year is 365 days or 52 weeks or 12 months long.

January is the first month of a new **year**.

yes

When you say yes, it means you agree with something.

Yes! I will fight Maleficent!

yesterday

Yesterday was the day just before today.

The rainstorm **yesterday** left puddles on the ground.

yoghurt

Yoghurt is a soft food that is made from milk, sugar and different flavourings, such as strawberry.

Yoghurt is a quick, healthy snack.

young

When someone is young, it means that person has not been alive for a long time.

Even when he was **young**, Arthur prepared to be king.

zebra

A zebra is a wild animal that looks like a horse with black-and-white stripes.

Zebras come from Africa.

zero

Zero is the number for nothing.

Zero comes before one.

0

zip

A zip has two rows of metal or plastic teeth that fit together when the zip is closed. They come apart when the zip is open.

This new winter jacket has a shiny **zip**.

zoo

A zoo is a place that you can visit where all kinds of wild animals live and are cared for.

Look what's happening at the **zoo**!

a b c d e f g h i j k l m n o p q r s t u v w x y